You Are Somebody
and I am, too!

You Are Somebody
and I am, too!

Mary Jane Holt

Mary Jane Holt
June 1, 2004

Enjoy!

Dream Catcher Publishing, Inc.

Copyright 2004 Mary Jane Holt
All Rights reserved

First Edition May 2004

Other Books by Mary Jane Holt

**From the Corners of my Heart
What IS Love?**

Library of Congress Control Number 2004104674

ISBN 0-9712189-5-3

Published by

**Dream Catcher Publishing, Inc.
P.O. Box 14058
Mexico Beach, Florida 32410
888-771-2800
www.DreamCatcherPublishing.net**

You Are Somebody
and I am, too!

DEDICATION

To the MCHS Class of 1966
– from whence I came –

OVERVIEW

You Are Somebody *and I am, too*! by Mary Jane Holt, offers the reader a tender and timeless view of human heart interaction throughout the author's beloved south and beyond. Following an 18 year career as a professional nurse, Ms. Holt took pen in hand in the fall of 1986 and hasn't put it down. A born and bred daughter of the south, an offspring of the Bible belt, she is somebody with an innate ability to make you know you are somebody, too. In the beginning, her goal was to find ways to heal through the written word. This native Georgian has done that and more. Her work has encouraged and entertained, challenged and educated. It is with a unique, earthy, and ultimately southern flare, that this writer shares her stories. **You Are Somebody** *and I am, too!*, primarily a collection of excerpts from Ms. Holt's award-winning newspaper column, will touch the hearts of readers around the world.

TABLE of CONTENTS

POEM: You Are Somebody

PART ONE - You and Yours
A Strange Sense of Timing – March 1987
Seeing a Sermon in Action – October 1987
Mr. Mac's Goodbye – December 1988
No Time to Wonder – April 1992
Three Days with Olga – March 1993
Tell Them Santa Sent You – November 1993
Milt's News – March 1994
What Makes for a Good Night's Sleep – March 1994
I Lied – July 1994
The Meeting Tree – October 1995
Canoeing through Amazing Grace – January 1997
My Friend Is Gone Now – January 1997
Being Remembered for Coming and Caring – March 1997
Deep and Delicate Themes Tug at my Heart – May 1997
You Never Know What Door a Smile Might Open – August 1997
Front Porches and Soda Fountains – October 1997
Greg Brezina – November 1997
You Better Hurry and Get Here – March 1998
While Monica Tells Her Story – August 1998
You Gotta Trust Me On This One – November 1998
Losing Lindsey at Christmas – December 1998
POEM: There Is Tomorrow
One Town, One Job, One with Those Served – August 2000
Single Parenthood – September 2000
A Piece of History – October 2000
Learning to Keep My Mouth Shut – November 2000
Terry Kay's "Voice Like God's" – August 2001
Paul Grice, Teacher – October 2001
Strangers Sharing Lunch – November 2001
Customer Service – August 2003
An Italian Influence – October 2003
Fairhope, Alabama – December 2003
Evander Holyfield – March 2004

PART TWO - Me and Mine
Remembering One's First Love – July 1991
The Drill Sergeant's Run – August 1991
The 1991 Class Reunion – August 1991
People Watching – November 1992
Oh, Missy, Be Careful – August 1993
It's Mother's Day Again – May 1994
Where the Wild Violets Grow – March 1995
On Picking Up Strangers – June 1995

The Surprise – November 1995
It Was Her Dumplings I Wanted – May 1996
Holding No Candle to the Likes of Her – June 1996
Where She Learned Simplicity – July 1996
Rejoicing Over Second Chances – August 1996
Because Your Load Looked Heavy – October 1996
Aunt Audrey – November 1996
POEM: Tomorrow Calls
Ending the Conspiracy – March 1997
My Princess Is Dead – September 1997
POEM: The Price
Being There for the Birthing and the Dying – November 1997
I Only Thought I Was Tough – January 1998
Empty Promises – February 1998
On Profanity and Morality – March 1998
Scratching Peg's Bellybutton at 4:30 A.M. – March 1998
The Accomplice – April 1998
What Snuffy Taught Me – September 1998
When Frankie Died – November 1998
Jim and Me – January 1999
Dylan and Me – January 1999
What My Heart Considers – March 1999
Is There a Doctor Aboard? – May 1999
Saving Sybil – March 2000
Elise and Me – March 2000
Following Sybil's Progress – March 2000
Meeting Sybil – April 2000
The Ultimate Frozen Stress Buster – July 2000
Telling It Like It Used To Be – July 2000
Some Doors Can't Be Closed – August 2000
Setting the Rooster Free – October 2000
Southern Lady in Black Jeans – December 2000
Building Mansions and Character – March 2001
Swamp Gravy – July 2001
Fresh Air Bar-B-Que - August 2001
Chocolate Sin – September 2001
Gene and Jimmy – February 2002
Soup and Lacy Corn Bread – February 2002
My Mama's Family – April 2002
The Underwear – April 2003
The 2003 Class Reunion – October 2003
The Vicks – December 2003
The Servant – February 2004
All Things Jesus – February 2004

IN CLOSING
POEM: What Only You Can Do

you are Somebody

i don't know any better
than to just go barging in
to peoples' lives
when they're hurting
'cause i've been there
and i've wondered
if somebody cared
so when i care
i try to show it
or how will they know it?
oh, sure!
i know there's always prayer
and i could just pray
that God would meet the need
and heed the cry of each aching heart
and do His part
to make it all better
and i could ask Him
to send somebody
to feed or clothe or comfort
but then
there was that time
i asked Him
to do just that for them
and He said to me
"you are Somebody"

PART ONE - You and Yours

A Strange Sense of Timing – March 1987

You know how life goes along and we live day after day, sometimes wondering how much of what we are doing is really right and profitable. Well, something wonderful happened to me recently and it seemed to put a stamp of approval on my lifestyle. Strange, but wonderful.

It was one of those mornings when I found myself doing things a bit out of the ordinary. I sensed that I was on a time schedule that had been pre-planned and I had not planned it. Yet I felt pressed to leave my house before making the beds or doing the dishes. I sensed a need to leave before I was actually ready to leave, so I did.

Driving toward Pace Warehouse in Forest Park to do some shopping, I continued to sense an awareness outside of myself. The route I took was out of the ordinary. I never drive by Clayton General Hospital, in Riverdale. Yet, I did that morning. When I reached Highway 19&41, I was a bit annoyed with myself for not turning off on the little road just past Cub Foods. No big deal, but there would have been less traffic if I had turned there.

So I drove through the busy intersection and up by K-Mart on Frontage Road which runs along beside I-75. Then I saw the wreck. It had just happened and I knew instantly that the people involved were the reason for my strange sense of timing and direction that morning. I pulled off the road and got out of my car, as did a young attorney in the automobile behind me.

A construction worker ran to the fence separating I-75 and the road we were on. I asked if anyone was hurt and he said, "Yes, a lady is bleeding and she is real white." The attorney left to call an ambulance and over the fence I climbed.

No one was stopping out on I-75. In fact, the cars were hardly slowing down and the wrecked van was over in the third lane next to the median. So, I breathed a prayer and went through the traffic to Mrs. Proffitt.

Grace Proffitt was her name. She and her husband were on their way back home to Ohio. She was bleeding from a cut on her leg, and she was very pale.

Whether it was instinct, or prior nursing experience, somehow I knew she'd be all right if she would just talk to me, so within seconds we were talking and laughing.

The police came.

The ambulance came.

And I went on my way.

But a couple of hours later, I drove back by the hospital to check on the couple. One thing led to another, and by late evening I had the two in my home for the night until relatives could come from Ohio to drive them home.

The next evening, as we and our new friends sat in the living room chatting about the events which had brought us together, Mrs. Proffitt said, "I could feel myself slipping and I knew I was going to faint when I looked out the window and saw somebody climbing the fence. It was a woman. She began to make her way through the traffic and I had to hang on to see what she was doing."

I was just on my way to meet a new friend.

Later, I received a thank you card from Mr. and Mrs. Proffitt's daughter in Michigan. She had written these words: "I have never doubted that God works in the lives of His children every day. I am so grateful that you responded to His urgings and thus were able to help my parents in a time of crisis. Thank you for your courage and your kindness in opening your home to them. Your actions are a gift I may never have the opportunity to personally return to you, but will hope to pass on in service to someone else in need."

That last line made my day! I suspect a lot of problems which plague our world could be solved if we were more willing each day to slow down and help a stranger in need. And just think, if the concept of "passing it on" could catch on and prevail... then oh, my what difference it could make!

Seeing a Sermon in Action – October 1987

I do not know what his credentials are or even if he has a degree. I don't know what seminary he attended or how long he has pastored the church I attended last Sunday night in South Georgia.

I do not even know how great his sermon might have been. I do know he was off to a good start before he exited the sanctuary abruptly. But never have I been more impressed with a pastor's actions.

There were several congregational hymns, at first, in a warmly worshipful atmosphere. Then, about ten minutes into the sermon, a young mother entered the sanctuary with a small child in her arms. With quivering chin she beckoned to a young man seated in front of me. He quietly stood up and followed her into the hall where, momentarily, sobs became audible to those of us remaining in the sanctuary.

There was a pause from the pulpit, then a few more words, followed by another pause. The pastor stopped his sermon, requested prayer for those hurting alone in the hall, then excused himself with these words, "Although there is more to this sermon and I would like to finish it, I feel I am needed out there more than in here." Then down the aisle and out the door he went.

The door closed quietly behind him and someone dimmed the lights. As the organist played softly, an indescribable sweetness and unity seemed to consume those present. With heads bowed, and hearts seemingly united as one, prayers went up for a brother and sister in distress. There was truly a sweet, sweet Spirit in the place.

It was about twenty minutes before the music stopped. Someone approached the pulpit with the announcement of the horrible tragedy which would touch so many. The young man who had been sitting in front of me was called out of the service to learn that his grandparents had been murdered earlier in the day.

I am stunned and distressed about the crime which occurred in my hometown only a few blocks from the hospital where I trained to be a nurse. I am saddened and angry to know a couple in their eighth and ninth decades of life had to face such a violent death.

But what lingers more vividly in my mind today, and perhaps in my heart forever, is the compassion I saw written on the face of a young pastor as he exited the sanctuary that night. He had no idea what was causing the heartache in the hall. He was just a shepherd taking action because members of his flock were hurting. He simply dispensed with protocol and went to their side.

As I write, a tear slips down my cheek. I think of pastors everywhere and of how often they have "been there" for so many. And I think of others who refuse to be bound by schedules and the expectation of the crowd – men and women, boys and girls who are willing to turn from the duty of the day to meet the need of the hour.

I am glad I visited Christ United Methodist Church in Albany last Sunday. Though prepared and hungry to hear God's Word taught that night, I came away with a greater blessing, because I had seen a sermon instead of hearing one.

Mr. Mac's Goodbye – December 1988

I called him "Mr. Mac." He had heard me on a radio talk show earlier in the year. I had heard he was dying and that he wanted to meet me. I went out to meet him at the lovely country home a few miles south of Bainbridge, Georgia where he lived with his daughter. He appeared to be merely skin and bones. So thin. I was scared to hug him, but hug him I did and he hugged me in turn. He was well past eighty with bright eyes and a quick wit, well read and eager to share his years of experience and wisdom. He was easy for me to get to know and love.

We visited several times between August and December. I often thought of him. He had hoped to go to Florida for the winter. I received a call a week or so before Christmas and was told he would like to see me again if I came south and could stop by during the holidays.

We went south. We stopped by. He was weaker and thinner. Though his breathing was labored and his discomfort quite visible, he wanted to talk. We listened.

Then I had to ask, "Mr. Mac, you have lived, haven't you? Really lived!"

"Oh yes, Hon," he whispered, "I have lived!"

Then we talked for a while of Christmas and the One who had come so long ago to offer hope to the living and the dying.

Finally I said, "Well, Mr. Mac, I'm one who lives too, and I believe in being open, honest and curious. We both know this is the last time we will see each other here, so I have a request. When you leave, if there is anyway you could whiz up through Fayetteville and just tell me goodbye, would you do it?"

"You bet," he chuckled weakly.

We hugged one last time, and then he proudly pushed himself up onto the side of the bed to see me off.

He died a couple of days later. There was a memorial service in Bainbridge, on the day before Christmas. On Christmas Day, the body was transported to south Florida for the funeral and burial which was set for the day after Christmas.

On Christmas night, we were sitting with friends around our dining room table. My husband and I were remembering Mr. Mac and talking about our recent visit with him. I laughed as I told my friends how I had asked him to zip though Fayetteville when it came time to leave and let me know he was on his way.

The phone rang and I answered. On the other end, the feeble but light-hearted voice of an old man said, "Have a happy Christmas."

He sounded far away, like we had a bad connection. "Have a happy, happy Christmas," he repeated.

"What? Who is this? I can barely hear you," I responded.

"Oh, I just wanted to wish you a happy, happy Christmas!" and he hung up.

I did too, and recounted his end of the conversation to a roomful of expectant guests. They all sat silently staring at me.

"Oh no! No!" I laughed. "I know what you are thinking, but I am quite sure the phone equipment up there would be better than that! I could barely hear him."

"You never know..." said Peggy, as the stillness in the room echoed her thought.

No Time To Wonder – April 1992
Colleen Mitchell's only thought was, "Is this how I am going to die?"

No time for retrospection. No time for wondering if her life had mattered – for regretting mistakes, celebrating right choices, brooding over failures, rejoicing over successes. No time to wonder who would love and cherish the man who had fathered the infant son who only recently had completed their circle of love. Certainly no time for her whole life to flash before her. Such contemplation would come later.

Only the one thought as the massive dump truck bore down on her, "Is this how I am going to die?"

Seconds later, wedged between the crumpled passenger's side of her new Explorer and the road sign on which her side of the vehicle had come to rest, her first thought was, "I have to get out of here before something else happens!"

So she climbed out. Cut, bruised and visibly shaken, but alive.

Alive. That's when all the thoughts started to come. Thoughts about being alive. About living. About living until she died...

I know about those kinds of thoughts, and I will bet most of you do, too.

The assurance of death becomes reality to all of us sooner or later. And, if we're lucky, it is only the fear that touches us, at first. Then, the reality that we should prepare to die. Then, death itself.

We may have a personal close call with the unwelcome visitor through an accident or disease. He may touch our lives when he calls on a close friend or relative. We may happen upon some tragedy or disaster where mangled and still bodies echo the emptiness that life left behind. All over the world, on any given day, death leaves numerous calling cards.

The point is none of us can live very long without becoming aware of how short life can be, how quickly it can end. And once such an awareness sets in, it starts to change us.

I was eleven years old, the oldest of five children at that time. Mother was at home with the others while my dad and I were out shopping. He had just bought groceries and placed all of the bags in the back seat and floorboard of the car. We were starting out of the grocery store parking lot when the accident almost occurred. I felt my dad's arm go across my chest to hold me in the seat (seat belts were non-existent then) and groceries flew all over the vehicle. But there was no collision.

Yet, I was shaken. Very shaken. I started crying and couldn't stop. My dad could not understand. "We're all right," he said, "Nothing's hurt except a few broken eggs in the back seat. Everything is all right. Why are you crying?"

I answered him immediately, "You just don't understand, I want to be living when I die!"

He laughed. He did not understand. I'm not sure he ever understood my remark, or how that incident, combined with several others, impacted my life forever. You see, I came to the conclusion at the ripe old age of eleven that death would not be so bad if I was living when I died. But, if I was not living, if I was not truly, truly living, then death would be a horrible thing to face at any age.

It took a few years to start to overcome my fear of death. Oh, yes, it took a while to learn how to live, to discover how to experience life – to feel it, to taste it, to become intimate with it. No, clearly I know it is in learning to live that I am learning how to die.

Slowly, I have come to realize that death is only a part of life, a door, perhaps, into another world. I am comforted by the courage I find to walk down all the wonderful avenues of life which open to me, by the excitement that comes with exploring the unknown, and by the fulfillment and security that is mine in knowing I do not walk alone.

Three Days with Olga – March 1993
Her name is Olga. She is from St. Petersburg, Russia, and she has been in America for five weeks. It is her first visit to our country.

She has come here with four people from Armenia, and three others from Russia, to learn about American economics. Olga is a physician. Her fellow travelers are in other professions: journalism, construction, computer technology, etc.

I have been privileged to spend only a little time with Olga. Three days she has been with me. Three days which have changed forever my concept of Russia, and, perhaps, the world. No longer do I envision the hard, expressionless faces of the people in a Soviet Union I was taught to fear as a child. I am surprised that my longstanding concept of Russia, and the Russian people, is so different from the reality Olga shares and exhibits.

She is beautiful and petite. She is filled with excitement and wants to know everything! She wants to taste all foods and loves desserts! She has driven a Mercedes, shot a pistol, driven a tractor, cut grass. She has attended a family reunion, a real Southern family reunion with more than a hundred family members present!

She is a woman not unlike American women. She is attractive, very neat and conscientious about her appearance. She is married and has an eighteen year old daughter, Victoria (Vickie).

Olga is well learned and highly educated. She actually grew up in a museum in St. Petersburg where her grandfather was the director. Always, she has loved to read and learn. Her early school years are spoken of with fondness. Then, after twelve years at the Institute, which included her internship and residency in gynecology and obstetrics, she is now the director of the OB/GYN department at one of only two private medical clinics in all of St. Petersburg.

During the month of March, Olga worked with the staff at Newnan Hospital and PAPP Clinic in Coweta County, Georgia. She spent time at the side of physicians in Newnan and Atlanta who have shared their techniques, ideas and business acumen with her. She has asked many questions about medical economics.

She and six of her countrymen were taken into the homes of families in the Newnan area for the past five weeks. One young Armenian man was the guest of a family in Atlanta. I was privileged to meet all of them three days ago. Without exception they are humbled and thankful for their experience, as are those of us who have been blessed to come to know them.

When Olga leaves she will take home with her, on cassette tape, the theme from "The Bodyguard." She is an avid Whitney Houston fan and wanted very much to see Whitney's movie while in America. She now is a Kevin Costner fan as well! Olga says her daughter and her daughter's friends will "flip out," as we say in America, over her new Whitney Houston tape.

But, it was with apparent sadness that Olga listened over and over again to Whitney sing "I Will Always Love You." I ask if she misses her husband of twenty years as the emotion remains fixed on her countenance long after the song ends. "Yes, but, I think of America when I hear this song..." she says.

Olga will return to her homeland with eagerness and excitement and page after page of notes. She has kept a personal journal to share with family and friends, and a business journal to share with professional colleagues. She is longing to tell of her many experiences in America. There is much to take home to those waiting to hear of this land. Mixed emotions reign. Enthusiasm and eagerness to go to her family are apparent. Thanksgiving and sadness at leaving all her new found friends also are felt.

My heart aches, too, along with the hearts of her hosts, Ron and Charlene Hall of Newnan and so many others who have been blessed, perhaps "changed" by her presence. We will miss her and truly, we will "always love her."

Tell Them Santa Sent You – November 1993
He'd had trouble with his truck not running smoothly for two weeks and suspected transmission problems. A friend recommended Sandford Transmission Services in Forest Park.

He took his truck there for a diagnosis. The manager asked a mechanic to drive it around the block and check it out. As the mechanic pulled back into the driveway the keen ear of the manager delivered a judgment. "There's nothing wrong with your transmission; you might want to drive it to Meineke Muffler over on Jonesboro Road and let those folks take a look," he said.

"Tell them Santa sent you," he added. There was no charge.

At Meineke, they looked and listened, but said nothing was wrong with his exhaust system. They assured him they would like to take his money, but there was nothing they could do for him. Again, no charge.

After the transmission and exhaust system were ruled out, a call to a friend over in Alabama led to a diagnosis. The gentleman was able to fix his truck himself at little cost.

In the meantime, a young man in a neighboring county was having trouble with his transmission. He had driven his vehicle to a local dealer and asked the service manager to look at, or let a mechanic check out his transmission and give him some idea about what was wrong.

He already had replaced the transmission fluid and filter with no improvement. The service manager said a payment of $35 up front would be required and the vehicle would have to be put on the computer. He would not allow one of his mechanics to listen to the young man describe his problem, a problem which was escalating by the hour as he had already been out of work for two days. Nor would he allow any of his staff to step out the door and take a look (or listen) at the ailing vehicle.

As luck would have it, the paths of the two men with automobile trouble crossed. The first man referred the second man to Sandford Transmission Services. By this time the young man's vehicle was not running smoothly enough to drive it the nearly 30 miles to the recommended transmission repair shop, so he called the manager and described his transmission symptoms over the phone.

The automotive technician told him to go look at the linkage from the carburetor to the transmission and, if it was off, how to fix it. If that was not the problem then the transmission would probably have to be rebuilt, he said.

The young man followed instructions. The linkage was off. He fixed it and his car is now running smoothly at little cost for repairs.

Santa had done another good deed.

Now, I don't know the exact identity of "Santa," or the precise location of Sandford Transmission Services or Meineke Muffler in Forest Park, Georgia; but my holiday hat goes off to the men at these places of business.

If you see them before I do, give them my best wishes for a deservedly joyous holiday season since they appear to demonstrate the spirit of giving year round. Also, you can tell them I know two gentlemen who are deeply appreciative of their professionalism, honesty, expertise and generosity – two men whose praise speaks louder than any paid advertisement ever will.

Milt's News – March 1994
One day, a couple of years ago, I saw a small poster in Abby Holbert's office at the News Daily; later, I saw it again in the composition department. Then, on yet another day I saw it in still another department.

Again, as is the case so many times when I discover priceless jewels of wisdom, the poster did not credit an author, but I believe the words originated with by W. Heartsill Wilson. Usually, I buy posters or write down quotes and stick them everywhere imaginable in my office because they inspire or encourage me. But the words I shall share with you today truly blessed me.

First, let me tell you about another quote. A number of years ago I read in my now worn and treasured copy of "Mountain Trailways for Youth" these words which were recorded by Mrs. Charles Cowman, "Only one life, 'twill soon be past; only what's done for Christ will last."

Those words impressed me tremendously. As the daughter of a minister, I was exposed to a great deal of suffering and death among church congregations. Also, our family was quite large – two uncles and an aunt on my dad's side of the family and ten aunts and uncles on my mother's side. In my late teens, when my grandparents died, I had more than two hundred first, second and third cousins.

Such a large family also lent its share of tragedy to those early years. Auto accidents, drownings, leukemia, cancer, heart disease, stroke…, all staked claims among folks I knew and loved well. So, death showed me early on how quickly it can claim the one life we have to live while here on earth.

Now, in my forties, with more than twenty years of nursing experience behind me, I am more aware than ever of how short life can be. Still, older friends tell me that I have yet to grasp the full impact of its brevity.

At any rate, though only a teen when I first read Mrs. Cowman's book, I was already aware of how suddenly death could claim a life. The years have added emphasis to the truth I recognized then.

And now, back to the words on the poster which prompted this line of thought. In all three departments at the News Daily I read:

"This is the beginning of a new day. God has given me this day to use as I will. I can waste it or use it for good. What I do today is very important because I am exchanging a day of my life for it. When tomorrow comes, this day will be gone forever, leaving something in its place that I have traded for it. I want it to be gain, not loss… good, not evil… success, not failure… in order that I shall not forget the price I paid for it."

A few days ago, Milt, a close friend, dropped by for an unexpected visit. He has always been quite healthy. In his late forties, easy-going, trim and a handsome man, he has a wonderful family and a great job. While we visited, he spoke at length of a puzzling problem that he has developed over the past six months. Gradually, he is losing muscle strength. Doctors have not been able to tell him what's causing the progressive weakness. Different theories have been proposed and Lou Gehrig's Disease was even explored as a possible diagnosis.

To date, my friend does not know what's wrong with his body. He does know, however, that life has taken on new meaning. It always does when we are faced with the uncertainty of it. Perhaps it is good to be reminded of how short life can be. To be reminded that we have only one life to waste, or use for good. To be reminded that with the dawning of each new day comes the opportunity to begin again.

What Makes for a Good Night's Sleep – March 1994
Sometimes, I long to strip away all the veneer in order to discover what lies beneath an outwardly strong and beautiful person, or group of persons.

What inspires another to live well, to do good, to be honorable, to survive – even thrive under desirable or less than desirable circumstances?

What are desirable circumstances? What are less than desirable circumstances? What is goodness?

I suppose the answers would vary among those asked. The wealthy man living off his family's money and the self-made millionaire would probably offer different answers.

The retiring blue collar worker who has labored hard all his life for another, and his former high school classmate down the street who has his own automotive repair shop, might offer contrasting explanations.

The young single mother of two who struggles at twenty four years old to hold down a job and a half, who has to pay more for another to care for her children than she can pay for food to feed her family of three, and who has what little sleep she can claim riddled with restlessness born of guilt over having done less than her best, may respond differently from the twenty four year old college graduate who is about to marry the love of her life, who will wait until they are comfortably established to have a family, and who is engulfed in an assurance (however real or false) that they are well on their way to living happily ever after.

The preschooler whose parents tenderly tuck him in at night to the echo of his favorite bedtime story more than likely will define goodness differently from the little one across town who shivers with his mom in search of warmth and security in the wee hours of the night in the back seat of an old abandoned car.

Yet, all may be good people. People who would willingly harm no one. People who would eagerly help those worse off than they are (and always there are those who are worse off). People who care about other people, about their welfare, their basic needs in life, even their happiness.

Yes, I know there are many people across our land and around the world who do not care. Their only concern is for themselves. Today, my concern is not for them. In fact, for just a little while – maybe, just for today – I don't want to think about them at all.

I want to consider those who do care. Those who live decent, honorable lives in spite of wealth or poverty, whether there is a solid family circle or no family at all, and regardless of status in the community and all the amenities which we sometimes assume make living a good life and doing good and being good a little easier.

You see, I am convinced that in every circle, in every corner of the globe, there are potentially good people. But, what substantiates my convictions? What is the key? What is the answer to goodness? Does being good have its own rewards? By what standards do we come by definitions and answers?

Turn where you will when such questions roll around in your mind. Today, however, I am drawn again to the recorded words of Jesus. I believe that He was man's best and God's best. He left us a road map to the good life. He left us to make our own choices about following it. Wealth, riches and power are not necessarily a means or an end to achieving it. I suspect that goodness is, in and of itself, its own reward.

I took the time recently to consider at length what Matthew wrote about Jesus and goodness in the 12th and 19th chapters of his Gospel.

In a nutshell, it all comes from the heart. If a tree is good, its fruit is good; if it's bad, then the fruit is bad. And so it is with men and women. Wealth and education and security as we define them, may have little to do with being good.

Check it out for yourself. Matthew writes of the man of great wealth and of the homeless one who didn't even have a regular place to lay his head. Both men sought to obey all the commandments (a great place to start if one desires to be good). One had peace. The other did not.

So, why be good if there are no guarantees? Not even a guarantee of peace. Good question, huh? There may be no guarantees of peace, but there's a real possibility for it. Not the kind that makes headlines, just the kind that makes for a decent night's sleep.

I Lied – July 1994

Jeff's mom died last week. When I went to the funeral home to express my sympathy I hugged my friend and he whispered, "You know how I feel, don't you?"

"Yes," I said softly.

Yet, as the word rolled so easily off the tip of my tongue I knew in my heart that I did not. No one could know how he felt and feels. No one can ever know.

I know how I felt when my mom died. I know how I felt when my dad died. I know how I have felt on a great number of occasions when other family members, friends, and former patients of mine have died. I know, but I did not understand my feelings. Still, I do not understand.

Every time, I felt differently. So, how could I possibly know how my friend felt and is feeling? I could not have predicted with any degree of accuracy how I was going to feel over the loss of my loved ones. In retrospect, I am amazed at the gamut of emotions which stirred in my soul as loved ones have been laid to rest. The days and months to follow each loss produced a continuous spectrum of emotion.

I do know that death has taught me the value of life – the value of living, that is. Not breathing, but living.

And what does living mean to me?

One thing it means is having an awareness of the feelings of others, and of my own feelings.

For a time, I thought that life was so very complicated. But that was when I was an academic student. Once I finished nursing school and lost my first patient, a thirty-year-old mother of two, I remembered what I knew as a small child.

Life, or living life, is so simple and easy. It's feeling and caring and showing it. It consists of sharing a glance, a smile, a hug, a word, a meal – with family, a friend, a stranger. Living is sharing what is uniquely mine with what is uniquely another's and being happy for the wondrous privilege of such an exchange. Living is being there for a friend when his mom dies and not knowing what to say or do or how to make it better, but just being there.

I didn't really know what to say to my friend's comment about my knowing how he felt. The little "yes" that I whispered was a lie and I knew it even as I said it. But I felt alive and thankful for the opportunity to share an embrace and just be there for a friend.

The Meeting Tree – October 1995
He has seen and heard it all. His heart has broken a thousand times, yet it has not become hardened. His eyes tell me that he still knows how to love, and his book assures me that he has hope. Hope for his people. Hope for the lost. Hope for the poor, uneducated, unattended – for those who lack support in the communities from which they rise or fall.

His name is Jesse Goodwin. His speech is rich with a thick Southern drawl. His humility bespeaks a great faith. He is real. He is retired now after many years as an intake counselor with a Florida juvenile court.

His grasp of "community" is astounding. He has felt the pulse of his people and found it to be an irregular beat that needs the attention of the Great Physician.

He cannot forget what he has observed. He cares, and will hope and pray always for a better life for those whose lives are tarnished in neighborhoods riddled with drug and alcohol abuse, violence and crime.

His book is not polished. Nor should it be. It is "The Meeting Tree" and it is the story of communities across our country who claim to support their own in the best ways they know how, but are finding that their best is not enough.

Jesse was born 55 years ago in Pampano, Florida. Although he succeeded in gaining a college education, two brothers were less fortunate. One is serving a long prison sentence. The other died from tuberculosis which he contracted while in jail.

The kind, wise gaze of this quiet author was like a magnet on the day I met him. His soft-spoken easy manner told me I should read his book. I'm glad I did.

His publisher told me that Jesse had inquired about how to get his book published at his local library. He learned about Prospector Press, located in the small town of Moore Haven, Florida, drove over and walked into the publisher's office with a 280 page, hand-written *in pencil* manuscript under his arm.

So unpolished was his appearance on the day they met that, at first, the publisher thought he was there to ask if he could cut the grass. Then they started talking.

While the gentle black man with the unforgettable eyes spoke of his background and his passion for his people, Denton Moore decided the rough manuscript was worth a read. Shortly thereafter, Moore decided it was worth being nominated for a Pulitzer Prize!

Jesse Goodwin wrote "The Meeting Tree" primarily for poor black parents, many of whom cannot afford to spend $9.95 for a book. *(If you buy this book, please consider passing it on to someone who cannot afford to buy it.)*

"The Meeting Tree" is a disturbing account of the way many black Americans live in the South. The author tells the story of a little boy, Patches, whose career began as a two-year old runaway, and ended as a 15 year old murderer. Unlike so many writers who strive only to expose, Jesse laces his pages with *instruction and hope*. It is a must-read for any one wanting to better understand southern African American history. Yet, it offers hope to individuals of every color.

Goodwin writes of how the "meeting tree," a benevolent tradition, has been hopelessly corrupted by a street culture based on crime in general and drugs in particular. His true stories tug at one's heart strings. They are based on his life experiences and on his many years as a counselor. They help explain why so many young people today are alienated and have become dangerous to themselves and society.

His explanations are not excuses, however. They are only explanations that bring a much needed understanding. With understanding comes hope. And on the wings of hope will come growth and change. May God grant us all more of the courage and compassion demonstrated so beautifully on the pages of Jesse Goodwin's life.

Canoeing Through Amazing Grace – January 1997
Normally, as a new year begins I am a bit more self-centered than I am today. Normally, I would be thinking of all the things I need to do this year to improve myself; considering what I can do to enhance relationships with family and friends; planning a bit more intensely, contemplating how I could improve production at work; gathering information for tax time.

Normally, I would be doing any number of things today, except pondering on God's Amazing Grace.

How marvelously sweet the sound!

How incomprehensible...

How phenomenal...

I fear to think, to try to imagine, or begin to comprehend where we all would be without God's truly Amazing Grace.

Normal is not a word I can apply to the present moment or to any of the thoughts that are dancing in and out of my mind and heart.

I am afraid a friend is dying and my heart is breaking.

It's not like it's a surprise. You are just never ready to let death take a loved one.

Oh, you may say you are... sometimes, the pain and suffering become so intense that you pray for a release. You pray for rest. For sleep that won't come. Mostly, you pray for peace, for the kind of calm that always accompanies any measure of God's Amazing Grace. You pray for it in abundance. And when it comes, you marvel. That's all you can do. You simply marvel.

A few years ago, I wrote a little poem that I thought was a bit too simplistic at the time the ink was flowing onto the paper. Childlike, I thought. Almost kindergartenish...

> Jesus loves us,
> this I know.
> Why He loves us,
> I don't know.
> But, tell me,
> what more
> do we need to know?

At times like this, however, such truth seems utterly profound. I find it is all I need to know.

A year or so ago, just after the weakness began to take its toll, my husband took our friend canoeing down the Ocmulgee. I never heard a grown man talk about anything on earth with such awe, such total rapture, as he did when he spoke afterwards of the experience. The trip was one of those things he had always thought he might do "if he ever had the time."

Our friend had worked for Delta Air Lines for nearly thirty years. He also had owned a successful landscaping business. He had a beautiful wife, two wonderful children and a dog. He loved his life. He had no complaints. Really, he had NO complaints.

He was kind of quiet, not really shy. Just quieter than most. He believed in hard work and honesty. A man of principles, devoted to family and friendship. And, oh, how he has always enjoyed the beauty and calm of the outdoors. But work and family obligations had kept him from doing some of the things he had always thought he might do "if he ever had the time."

As his wife sat on the edge of their bed last night, head throbbing, eyes swollen, tears flowing, she kept whispering softly, "He doesn't deserve to suffer like this..."

No, I thought, he doesn't deserve the inescapable agony that accompanies Lou Gehrig's Disease at any stage and especially in the last months. No one does.

And then I remembered the one thing that makes times like this bearable: Jesus loves us. He loved us enough to die for us, to die alone that we may never be alone in life, or in death.

As he struggled so miserably for air and rest, I whispered to my friend "Whenever it gets bad like this, whenever you start to feel the panic, let yourself float down the river again. But this time, leave my husband behind and let Jesus handle the oars. Just rest and float and see the sights with Jesus as your Guide."

I thought even as the words rolled too smoothly off my tongue, "How simplistic, how easy for you to say."

But this morning, as I type this column, I know my words were not so simplistic after all. I remember that storm so many long years ago, in which the disciples feared for their lives while their master slept. When their panic forced them to wake Him and express their fears, He calmly spoke three words that would change forever the course, not only of that little boat, but of their lives and ours, "Peace, be still..."

I suspect that Jesus, Master of all the stormy waters of our lives, surely can manage another majestic canoe ride down the Ocmulgee and eventually across the Jordan. God's Amazing Grace assures me He can.

My Friend Is Gone Now – January 1997
My friend died this week.

After he had drawn his last breath, within a short span of minutes, maybe an hour or two, any number of spoken phrases danced in and out of my consciousness.

"He is in a better place."
"He is better off."
"Heaven has another angel, now."
"He doesn't have to suffer anymore."
Etc. Etc. Etc.

Yet, all I could feel, think, and say is, "My friend is gone."

At some point, perhaps I can consider more readily what was best for him. For now, I only feel a tremendous loss.

I wish I could tell you about the wonderful the Hospice program was in which he was enrolled, but I cannot. Words escape me.

Enrolled? Yes, I suppose that is as good a choice of words as any. Milt chose the Hospice route, so I suppose I can say he enrolled himself in their program.

Yet, it was not their program, but his own which he followed. He called the shots. The social workers, nurses, sitters, volunteers and all who were involved in his life over the past six or seven months were there to make him as comfortable as possible, to meet all needs that could be met. They did what they were called upon to do so beautifully, lovingly, and tenderly.

Milt had opted early on in his battle with Lou Gehrig's Disease not to have a tracheotomy, feeding tubes, intravenous feedings or any heroic resuscitation measures once the end loomed near. He chose instead to live well the days that were his to live "normally."

During the summer and early fall, he attended all of his son's ball games; even going with the team to the playoffs. He pushed himself to be there to watch, to silently cheer, to enjoy his son's activities.

Then every weekend, beginning in October, buddies drove him to the hunting camp he had shared with them for more than twenty years. They built a ramp for his wheelchair, set up a generator for his oxygen and put a comfortable recliner in place so he could be where he wanted to be, and do what he wanted to do, with as much ease as possible.

I remember clearly how depressed he was in January of 1996, so certain was he at that point that he would never get to enjoy another hunting season. Not that hunting mattered so much to him. Instead, it was being close to nature, "to God," he would say. He liked the camaraderie and the camp fire, too. Nobody ever enjoyed a camp fire quite like Milt did.

On a Sunday evening, only a few weeks ago, we had him down at our farm in Meriwether County. Long after the wieners and marshmallows were toasted and tasted, well after all the stars had come out, and even after those of us who had to go to work the next morning had begun counting the hours till dawn, Milt wanted "one more log" thrown on the fire.

He taught us much about beauty and patience. He never complained. Never. He never asked "Why me?" At times, he was frustrated when he would be "ready to go" and, for some reason, his illness would level off again, and he would realize it wasn't time yet. He learned to go with the flow and to bask in the glow from the flame of life.

Only in recent weeks did the tears begin to flow. But they never overshadowed his sense of humor, optimism and love of life. On the contrary, the tears only seemed to cleanse him in some way, or ways, of any imperfections that remained.

Milt, and others like him, were the reason I most enjoyed nursing. He and they were also the reason I left the profession ten years ago. The dying became too hard. In many cases, terminally ill individuals are afforded the time to learn to accept. We who minister to them often are too busy to learn to accept. The pain is compounded with each loss. Sometimes it gets to be a bit too much.

Yet, it is from the dying that I have learned the most invaluable lessons about living. We are the lucky ones who cross their paths as they grasp the true meanings of perspective, reality and life. When they sprinkle a bit of truth's dust at our feet, we must find the courage to walk on.

But more than finding the courage to walk on, we must take the time to slow down, throw "one more log" on the fire and enjoy the golden flame of life with those we love before it's too late.

Being Remembered for Coming and Caring – March 1997
Earlier this week, in an Associated Press Article, Dan Sewell quoted Rev. George Naylor in Kentucky:
``This isn't the time for theologizing or philosophizing about why," said Naylor, who served 10 years as pastor of the Falmouth Baptist Church until moving after 1992. ``I just give them hugs and let them cry. That's about all that can be done right now."
Did the pastor say a mouthful, or what?
Time will record his actions. He will be remembered for coming, for caring, for being there.
Sewell's article was about the flooding in Kentucky. It could just as easily have been about the tornadoes in Arkansas, or any number of places around the nation, or world, that have been touched by natural disasters in recent days and months.
What do we say?
What can we do?
Sometimes, giving hugs and lending a shoulder is all we can do.
Sure, food must be delivered, donations made, and hammer and nails put to good use. But when pain is sharp, as tears flow, hugs count.
I remember vividly my visit to Montezuma, Georgia in 1995. The main street is where the Flood of the Century hit the little town hardest, in 1994. Carl Adams' real estate office was only one of the businesses along the street that was shut down abruptly and for many long weeks after the waters came sweeping down the street.
"It was eerie," Adams told me. "Within three hours my office was flooded. We had no time. We had to leave everything and just get out."
Twelve feet is how high the waters got around his place. According to Adams, it wasn't the expected flow of the river that

drowned the little town for a season; it was the water flow caused by all the dams that broke north of the area. "Everything happened so fast and then the water was just coming and coming," he said.

Afterwards, when the waters had started to recede, the people started coming, too. They came from all over the country. A preacher, his wife and 22 members of his congregation came from a little church in Tennessee. In two days time, they put up all the insulation and hung new sheetrock in the real estate office.

All up and down the street, for months, strangers worked along with the townspeople to rebuild Montezuma. Folks in the old Georgia town have nothing but praise for the Salvation Army. One gentleman went on and on about all the Red Cross did, "It was amazing. They served us three meals a day from a food wagon. Didn't charge anything. Just went up and down the street, morning, noon and night, passing out food to all of us. I never saw anything like it."

Some of the townspeople told me they wouldn't have made it if it had not been for the Mennonite community of Macon County. They just took charge and were a tremendous help for area business and families. They set up a warehouse at an old mobile home manufacturing site and that's where all the donations were stored. Their organization was amazing. Lumber companies from all over the country sent free lumber to the folks in Montezuma. Building supplies were shipped from Macon at no charge. One company from Atlanta sent tractor trailer rigs with pressure washers and fans to clean up homes and businesses.

"And nobody would let us pay them," Adams said over and over.

I left Montezuma recalling the early years of American history. Neighbor helping neighbor was the best way to survive and thrive. It was a time when communities came together to build and rebuild.

As bad as it is when homes are ripped from foundations, businesses are destroyed, and loved ones are wounded or killed, it is still good when strangers offer help.

Whether it's in Tennessee, Kentucky, Ohio, West Virginia or Georgia, the pain is the same. So is the sense of thanksgiving when help comes.

Mr. Adams told me about a stranger who drove into town and parked his pickup out in front of the real estate office. Then the man who said he was from Valdosta walked in alone and calmly said, "I'm here to help. What can I do?"

For 12 hours that day and the next, he worked along with the other strangers who had come to give aid. They tore out walls and flooring and cleaned mud from every nook and cranny of the main street office. When they had to leave, miraculously, others appeared to lend a hand. It was as if some master engineer was overseeing the entire project, sending just the right people at the right time to do the most good.

I know, like me, you probably have wondered, if there is a Master Engineer, why did He ever let all the devastation happen in the beginning? I think the minister in Kentucky was on to something when he said, ``This isn't the time for theologizing or philosophizing about why, I just give them hugs and let them cry. That's about all that can be done right now."

Deep and Delicate Themes Tug at my Heart – May 1997

Among the cover quotes printed on the back of "Praise Jerusalem!," by Augusta Trobaugh, you will find the following words from Terry Kay, native Georgian and author of "To Dance with a White Dog:" "I do not expect to read anything this year more evocative or more charming than "Praise Jerusalem!... This beautifully, poetically written novel is another abundant harvest from the rich fields of Southern literature."

Knowing well Terry and his own work, and being aware of what an avid reader he is, I will admit his statement hooked me, almost instantly.

Unprepared for the tremendous range of emotion I would feel as I turned the pages, I was torn between reading it straight through in a day or two, and stretching it out over a week or so. In the end, I stretched it out – I wanted it to last like a box of fine chocolates that are just too good to wipe out in one sitting.

"Praise Jerusalem!" transported me back to another place and time. A simpler time. A quieter time. Maybe even a happier time, in some ways. Though the novel revolves around only a few short weeks in the lives of three women in rural Georgia, its deep and delicate themes tugged at more than one corner of my heart.

Miss Amelia, Maybelline and Mamie take us back to a time of coloreds and whites, Camp Meetings, small town aristocracy and coming of age. They bid us feel with them the prejudice, the electricity, the fear of losing status, security, and the precious things of our lives, as well as the exhilaration of discovering that which cannot be taken from us.

The unlikely threesome teach us about survival in its finest form, and they do it with great flair. As they journey together they enlighten us. Through their revelations about themselves they lead the reader to discover more than some of us might care to know about ourselves. Yet their discoveries pave the way for a deeper understanding of their time and ours.

As their lives become entwined, the Great Mystery starts to unravel. And never have I seen, heard, or enjoyed a better unraveling of the Great Mystery. "Praise Jerusalem!" is for searching hearts everywhere. It's what this writer recommends heartily for anybody who needs lessons in letting go, forgiving, growing and loving. Ever so intriguing from cover to cover, I predict "Praise Jerusalem!" will prove to be another timeless work of art.

Author Augusta Trobaugh earned a Master of Arts degree in English from the University of Georgia with a concentration in American and Southern literature. Her work has been funded by the Georgia Council of the arts and "Praise Jerusalem!" was a semi-finalist in the 1993 Pirate's Alley Faulkner competition.

"Praise Jerusalem!" is worth checking out.

While I'm busy again at suggesting you check out things, I suppose this is as good a time as any to break down and tell you about the cafe in Concord. I won't go into any great detail since space won't permit, and as always, I am a bit reluctant to tell others about extra special things and places I'd really rather selfishly keep to myself.

But, if you are ever down toward Concord on a Sunday around noon, you must – and I do mean absolutely must – check out the buffet at the Concord Cafe. You mustn't expect anything fancy, just some of the best down home vittles in Georgia.

And don't be in any big hurry if you ever do mosey down that way. Go early for lunch and enjoy the afternoon. The surrounding countryside is a sight to behold. Where "Praise Jerusalem!" will allow your heart and soul to stroll down Memory Lane, the little town of Concord will let your feet do the same.

This quaint little town of yesteryear is west of Griffin, south of Jonesboro and Fayetteville and east of Newnan, almost in the heart of middle Georgia. You have to look close on the map to find it.

If you do have the inclination and find the time to seek out Concord, I suggest you make your way across to Gay or Woodbury and on towards Greenville or Warm Springs. Then again, you might want to save Warm Springs for another day. You can spend a whole day there visiting all the shops and you should eat at The Bullock House, known far and wide for its expansive buffet served amidst just the right touch of country elegance! Of course, you cannot do The Bullock House if you are full from the Concord Café! It's easy to leave both places thinking you would be wise not to eat again for a week, but the visits are worth it!

Oh, and Callaway Gardens lies only a few miles west of Warm Springs, but you should dedicate a whole day, or a long weekend, or even a week to see the Gardens. Actually, some folks rent cabins there for months at the time.

Okay, back to that Sunday afternoon ride I was suggesting. Be sure to take snacks and beverages in a cooler and don't worry about road numbers, just drive. If you really want to add a new dimension to lazy Sunday afternoon fun, then enjoy the excursion with a friend or relative and take turns choosing which way to turn when you come to each intersection.

Just be sure you have a good map when it's time to turn back towards home (and don't sneak a peek at it until then). That way you can figure out where you are and how to get back to where you've come from. That feat in and of itself is its own reward!

Words will never adequately describe the vast and glorious wealth of our great state, but works of art like "Praise Jerusalem!" and magic Sunday afternoon drives to out-of-the-way places like Concord have a way of scratching the surface.

You Never Know What Door A Smile Might Open – August 1997

Her name was Amy and if Clayton County offered a Smile of the Week Award she would be in the running. Assuredly, she would receive my vote.

I had been in and out of the rain all morning. I had skipped breakfast because low grade fever, aching muscles and a terrific headache tends to take away one's appetite. The morning had grown long as I met several necessary obligations. I had one more stop to make, but decided I must take a break and try to eat a bite.

For a half hour or so I mulled over what might taste good under the circumstances. Nothing, I surmised at first. Then I thought of Schlotzsky's Deli. The sandwiches those folks put together seem to taste good any time. Why not? Hot chicken soup was not to be found, so I decided to go for a Schlotzsky's special on sour dough bread.

I would have been happy enough to just enjoy a good sandwich in a quiet, clean setting, but I was in store for more than that during my visit to the little Riverdale eatery. I received a wonderful, almost electric, day-changing smile from a beautiful young woman who seemed to exude sincere interest in her customers.

She said hello and took my order efficiently which is all I expect in most restaurants. But she did it with a special warmth and friendliness. No hint of boredom or irritation. Nothing to make you think she was there only long enough to put in her time and make a little money.

Nope, I promise you she seemed happy. And her happiness danced on the waves of the smile she bestowed on her customers. It was hard not to feel better as I watched her interact with other strangers who came through the door. She will go places, I thought, and that smile will open the special doors of her life for more than one adventure.

Time was when just about everybody I knew smiled. In rural Georgia, some still do. They even throw up their hands and wave a greeting when you pass on the highways. And they still drive slowly enough that you can actually see the gesture and return it! Yet, more and more of us are living too fast to smile anymore, aren't we? Couple our daily pace with the fear of strangers that now indwells most of us and you have a setting where smiles could become a lost art.

I hope Amy hangs on to hers. And I trust that her bright eyes, and inquisitive mind and heart, will continue to serve her well throughout life. I was glad she took my order so warmly. It made a bad day better.

I often have suspected that it was the smile of a now famous Georgia peanut farmer that opened the door of the White House for him. Still, it opens doors for him all over the world. His smile also is electric, almost magnetic. It draws you into who he is and what he's doing. It makes you want to know more about him and his projects. Perhaps it laid the foundation for the first house he built for the poor. It probably graced the first passport that took him into impoverished nations where his influence continues to make a difference today.

I think history will deem Jimmy Carter one of the truly great political leaders of the twentieth century. Yet, prior to 1976, this peanut farmer who had been a naval officer, as well as governor of Georgia, actually stood outside the main power groups of the Democratic Party. I think it was that smile of his that allowed him entrance into the hearts of Americans everywhere.

After he gained the party's nomination and defeated President Gerald Ford in the election of 1976, President Carter brought together the heads of the governments of Israel and Egypt to sign the historic peace treaty of 1979, reestablishing diplomatic relations between their two countries. But personally, Carter was, and is, known for his informality, his bright smile, and his work among the impoverished of this land and beyond.

You just never know what a beautiful, God-given smile that radiates from a warm and caring heart, will do for the one who wears it or the one who sees it. Only history knows, and it doesn't give previews. Keep smiling, Amy!

Front Porches and Soda Fountains – October 1997

What a month! Hope yours has not been as stressful as mine. If it has, then for goodness sakes, put the brakes on! We can only stand so much, you know.

It's time to "chill" as my spunky young friend and niece, Michelle, is fond of saying. Cool it, calm down, relax, just let go of the tension, TAKE A BREAK. Whatever the word, whatever the means, sometimes we just have to get off the merry-go-round for a while. An hour, a day, a week.

A week? Not hardly, but it's a nice thought!

I did claim an hour on Monday of this week, however. While out on an assignment that was going every which way but well, I drove by Eagle's Landing Pharmacy in Stockbridge, and remembered the soda fountain inside! I cannot, do not, and will not allow myself to pass up soda fountains. Not ever!

Besides, it was lunch time, and I deserved a taste of the best ambiance in town. A break was most definitely in order, and the chance to step back in time could not have come at a more appropriate moment.

So, I braked, and turned my car around to head back. I was anxious for the old drug store soda fountain scene to welcome me once more. It did, and again I found it could not be beat for price, taste, or company. It's where I met Ben Stephens this time. Of course, I always meet nice people at soda fountains; it's the one place you know it's still okay to talk to strangers!

I sat down in front of the covered cake stand that was laden with plump chocolate chip cookies, struggling to maintain some degree of discipline, and order just the chicken salad sandwich and a sweet iced tea. Then I looked to my right and saw one of those newfangled digital phones that's like a walkie-talkie, pager, and telephone all in one, laying on the counter just two stools over.

What a sad invasion, I thought to this wonderful old lunch counter. But the 20th century rules – the 90's no less – so I considered turning to the owner and asking about the phone. I was curious to talk to somebody who had used one for a while. I had stopped twice in recent weeks to discuss with a local marketing representative how this latest in portable communication devices might assist me in my work, and at what cost.

Should I take advantage of the opportunity to gain first hand, unbiased information even if the gentleman to my right had dared lay the noisemaker atop the only monument around that reminded us of simpler times?

Sure, I thought, so I struck up a conversation with Ben Stephens, assistant vice president of HomeBanc Mortgage Corporation. Warm and friendly, he readily outlined a number of positives and negatives about the menacing little black phone that lay before us.

I should have known right off that Ben hailed from South Georgia, but we were well into conversation before he verbalized the fact. Not that north or middle Georgia natives are not friendly; it's just that there is something about South Georgia folks, something you can't quite define, something that's almost always a tad warmer and friendlier.

We talked at length during a too brief lunch break. Afterwards, I drove away trying to remember the words to the "if the world had a front porch" song by Tracy Lawrence that I had heard so often on WKHX out of Altanta. It had recently lingered long near the top of the country music charts. I let myself wonder for a brief moment about what a better place our world might be if front porches and soda fountains could somehow make a comeback.

But duty called, and I had to let go of my wonder... until two days later when I was opening my mail and came upon a delightful note from my new friend, Ben Stephens. He wrote, "Thanks for starting up a conversation at lunch on Monday. I think you are right about soda fountains and lunch counters. If we had a few more around we could probably get most of the world's problems solved."

His note reminded me once again that not only do you meet nice people at soda fountains, since it's one place you know it's still okay to talk to strangers, but, if you are lucky, you walk away knowing it's true that "a stranger is just a friend you don't know yet."

Greg Brezina – November 1997
After retiring from professional football in 1980, former Atlanta Falcon Greg Brezina, and his wife Connie, founded Christian Families Today. They have worked almost tirelessly for the past couple of decades to save America's families.

What a calling! Notice I said almost tirelessly.

Bear in mind, as I tell you about Greg, God makes no mistakes! God knew well the man he called to minister to breaking and broken families nearly 20 years ago. Just like he knew Moses and Elijah and Peter and John and Paul, God knew Greg.

When I first met him in early 1982, I was more than a little impressed with Greg's commitment to sharing the Gospel. It could be no other way, for this record breaking linebacker had come face to face with the supreme quarterback of all time. On opposing teams for many years, the day Christ threw him the Good News of Salvation, Greg caught it and has been running with it ever since.

Assuredly, however, that throw and catch was no accident, for I am as certain as day follows night that God called this dynamic athlete off the football field and placed him front and center in the great game of life – the one where saving the soul of mankind is the ultimate goal.

Over time, saving America's marriages and families became the theme of Greg and Connie's life. And since you and I both know what a challenge that is, it is easy to understand how Greg grew tired.

But there is another reason for the fatigue that began to overtake him. Recently, Greg admitted that the Christianity he had experienced for 20 years "has been like a roller coaster – full of emotional highs and lows, and with little rest." He said he would rise early in the morning, have a two hour quiet time, feel good and be on top, then sin, feel guilty, and plunge to the bottom. Afterwards, he would confess, promise God he would try harder, then sin again. He said the never ending cycle was physically draining. Been there? Me, too! That's why I have to tell you about what has happened to Greg.

First, I want you to know that in a dream I had about twelve years ago, Greg walked into my yard carrying a large black Bible and crying "Obedience." Yeah, just "obedience" and holding God's Word high in the air. It was that dream that set me on the course I now travel and I will never cease to be thankful for the way God uses Greg Brezina and other men and women who are not afraid to take up their cross and follow Jesus Christ.

For with obedience comes peace. And peace is awesome...

I feel confident that Greg's efforts to obey are as sincere as any truly committed Christian. But we still live in human bodies and the battle within never ends. It is that battle that can lead to the fatigue, weariness and depression. The only thing that can free us from the vicious cycle, and let us off that roller coaster of performance and failure, is God's grace. As Greg has grown in God's grace, he has learned to rest in the reality of what he has learned that it means to be "in Christ."

His joy and peace is as blatantly apparent now as was his restlessness for many years. You may wonder if Greg's sin was so great that it blocked the peace and rest he longed for. Not hardly. Greg Brezina is a man of God if there has ever been one. But, like Peter of old, he has had his growing pains. And also, like Peter and others before and after him, Greg has come face to face with grace so great that it has changed him again.

But only in God's time. You see, Greg and Connie and a great number of other individuals are working to establish Still Waters, a retreat near Lake Oconee in middle Georgia. Still Waters will be open to those who need rest from time to time, *and* need to be reminded anew, or told for the first time, of God's amazing grace.

I suspect that if Greg had not traveled the road he has traveled since 1980, and known the weariness he has known, he would never have begun to understand and appreciate so completely the utterly remarkable miracle of transformation that takes place as we grow in grace. Such is the way God works in all out lives.

Christian Families Today remains as committed as ever to working with couples and families who need to be encouraged. But something new has been added. "Grow in Grace" seminars are now offered as well. Check it out at www.cftministry.org.

You Better Hurry and Get Here – March 1998
I have been wanting to meet Gina Weathersby for months. When we finally had lunch this week, we talked forever.

Gina founded Aging Matters, a company which assists families in planning for elder care and all types of "aging matters." She feels like many folks don't begin to live until age 60, and with proper planning, those wonderful years can be even better. On the other hand, she recognizes that many individuals, even as young as 60 years of age, need specialty care – care that they may not know how to find.

I was so intrigued to hear how Gina decided to start her company. Her story reminded me of my sister Lynda. You know how I talk about Lynda always being there for the birthing and the dying. "It's a family thing," she says.

Well, Gina nursed her grandmother off and on for a decade. For a number of years, she flew back and forth from Charleston to attend to her. Eventually, however, Grammy came to live with Gina and her family in Georgia. As she became more and more feeble, her children were forced to place Grammy in a nursing home. Still, Gina went to see her every day. As the end drew near, it became somewhat exciting.

One day, Grammy called Gina and said, "You better hurry and get here. I think it's coming."

I think it's coming... Grammy thought it (death) was coming, and she wanted her granddaughter there to share it with her. Actually, death did not come on that particular day though Gina had hurried, as requested, in order to be there for Grammy, the way Grammy had always been there for other family members. Yet, when the time of passing did come, Gina was there. Today she recounts the experience as a very special one.

Over lunch we talked at length about the joys of sharing special moments with loved ones. (Yes, dying can be a very special time.) I recalled a patient I cared for at one time who was so terribly depressed because she had cancer and knew she had only a few weeks or months left. She was not depressed, I told Gina, because she knew she was dying, but because her family was still in denial and would not let her talk about it. And she needed to talk. Through her illness she had learned much and wanted to share some of what she had gleaned. Also, she was ready to start saying goodbye. She did not want to wait until the very end when communication may become more strained, perhaps impossible.

I have maintained for a number of years that only the dying know how to live. Of course, we are all dying from the moment we are born, but not everyone accepts the fact, faces it, deals with it. Those whose physicians pronounce them terminally ill are often forced to confront the issue. Those who have had near fatal accidents frequently come away changed forever. There's just something about looking death square in the eye that puts a whole 'nother perspective on many things.

I will forever be grateful to so many individuals who have shared their insights on living and dying with me. Dying is not always a happy experience for the one doing it, or for those who share the time, but it is made far more bearable when families plan for it, and when the dying one is at peace with God, and his or her fellowman. I am thankful for Gina and others like her who help individuals and families plan for the inevitable, and work through countless challenges as the time of dying approaches.

Remember, life can be what passes us by while we are making plans for "some day." Learn to live every day as if it were your last. The effort will make a difference for you and all those who share this journey with you. Don't just look, learn to truly see. Don't just hear, learn to really listen. Don't just reach, reach out and touch. Don't just celebrate things or events, celebrate <u>life</u> with those you love.

While Monica Tells Her Story – August 1998
He's 79 years old. She's 78. He has Alzheimer's Disease, and though she will admit to a great many "problems" over the past five years, he has not been a burden. Not ever.

He took a fall a few weeks back. Found the key to the basement door (it's kept locked at all times for his safety), opened it and tumbled down the stairs. Broken bones and a bruised kidney sent him reeling for days, hanging in the balance between life and death while double pneumonia made the rules.

As his family kept constant vigil, the doctors routinely agreed and disagreed about his prognosis. Finally, he was released to a nursing home where he must be fed, diapered and cared for constantly. A successful save according to one doctor. A shame according to others.

She is crying almost constantly. She never wanted him to be in a nursing home. Never. But she feels she has no choice...

All this while Monica bargained for immunity.

A Fayette County, Georgia teen died recently in a fiery sports utility vehicle crash while five sheriff's deputies fought overwhelming flames to try to save him. Their small car fire extinguishers were no match for the consuming blaze. The efforts of those officers and the four county and city fire vehicles that responded to their call for help could not extricate the youth.

The young man is believed to have lost control of his vehicle while traveling at a high rate of speed around a corner just south of Bethea Road in Fayette County. The vehicle reportedly went down an embankment through some smaller trees before impacting a larger tree. The vehicle came to rest approximately 20 feet from the edge of the road in a wooded area as flames engulfed it.

Fiery entrapments are extremely tough for emergency crews, and almost unbearable for the surviving families of the victims. I am told that tragedy has repeatedly struck the family who experienced this horrendous loss. My heart aches for the mother of the young man as I am sure her heart must be breaking. At times like this, one wonders how one can go on. It is only God's grace that assures us we can...

All this while Monica prepares to testify before the grand jury.

Powerful bombs explode outside the U.S. embassies in Kenya and Tanzania. A four-story building is toppled and more than 50 people are killed. Officials claim early on that more than 1,000 are injured, including the American ambassador to Kenya.

Rescuers made their way through crumbled concrete and tangled metal bars, in attempt to reach dozens of trapped people. The Red Cross reported that more than 40 people were killed and more than 1,000 wounded in Nairobi alone. As rescue efforts continue, other victims are expected to be found...

All this while Monica recovers from a grueling day before the grand jury.

The stock market bounces up and down like a seesaw while some compare the present activity to that of the pre Nixon resignation days. We rejoice over our gains and grieve over our losses as big business responds to poor Monica's plight.

I am having trouble believing what I am writing today. Aren't you? Can it be that America has once again allowed itself to hang by the threads of still another scandal. Must our stability as a nation always rest on the laurels or losses of the rich and/or famous? I am sick of hearing about Monica's struggles. I am fresh out of concern for a president who struggles to figure out how to tell the "truth" or yet another version of it.

What about the many citizens of this land, in my community and yours, whose day to day conflicts define real struggle?

Many believe the cocktail dress will tell all. Talk is that our president will eventually admit to all accusations, explain how he had to lie to protect his family, ask for forgiveness and America will forgive. Can life get any more sordid? Could we send any more pathetic message about morality to the youth of this land and the world?

There are too many people out there who deserve our sympathy and concern. Near and far they need our prayers. We must be about the business of caring for those who truly crave and deserve our time and attention. We may never make it into the Oval Office for personal visits with the president, but perhaps we, too, will one day be called upon to give an account of how we spend our time.

You Gotta Trust Me On This One – November 1998

Would you agree there are things, many things, that we own, or *think we own*, that we would not want to lose or misplace? Eyeglasses would be on that list. Close to the top. I've lost them many times. Usually they are sitting right on top of my head or tucked into my blouse the whole time I'm frantically looking for them. When some kind soul finally asks what I'm looking for, and tells me where they are, I remind myself that the glasses were, of course, totally out of my line of vision. Thus, I don't feel quite so stupid.

My car (surely you've walked out of the mall or grocery and been unable to remember where you parked!), the car keys, a favorite lipstick, and any number of other things have found their way to my list of things forgotten over the years. But just now, I am terribly irritated with myself for losing something that means a great deal to me. Actually, it's not lost. I put it somewhere special where I would not get it mixed up with my other note pads.

You've been there too, huh? You would think we would learn that routine storage is not always bad. Those special places will trip us up every time.

So, while my writing pad, with all my notes from my interview with Ralph Emery, lies hidden in its very safe place, I must try, from memory, to tell you about an interview I did with him in September. I could wait until the pad turns up I suppose, but then you might miss your chance to meet this truly special gentleman. He will be in Atlanta, at the Peachtree Battle Store of Chapter 11, on December 5, at 7 p.m. signing his latest book, "The View From Nashville."

The book is more than deeply entertaining for this country music fan who grew up with the songs of Loretta Lynn and Conway Twitty. Delightfully easy reading takes you into the hearts and lives of many of country music's greatest stars as only the author can.

Why is that? Why do I feel that Ralph Emery can tell us what we want to know better than anyone else?

As I wonder about that for a moment, I realize I don't need my notes at all to tell you what matters about Ralph Emery. The man is all heart. He cares... He is totally void of arrogance. You gotta trust me on this one. There is not one shred of arrogance in this fellow, just an awesome appreciation for life and all those with whom he is lucky enough to share his days on earth.

He exhibits a tremendous curiosity about people and what motivates them. He wants to know all about where they've been and where they are going. Thus, it was a challenge for this writer to keep him talking about himself for two hours. In fact, it was almost impossible. He could not understand my interest in him.

Can you believe it? I was more than interested. I was intrigued by this man who has almost single-handedly made stars out of so many country music greats. In his early years, as an all night DJ on WSM in Nashville, he was often the first to bring us the music. I remember well that powerful voice coming over the airwaves to introduce the songs I grew up on. Then, with Nashville Now and The Ralph Emery Show, he brought us the stars themselves. He continues to do this through On The Record, seen weekly on TNN. I'm not sure anybody can conduct a better interview. Not even Barbara Walters.

Why? Because his questions come so smooth and easy. It's like he does not have an agenda. Like his guest is the only person in the universe who matters at that moment in time. Like he really wants to know them – not just conduct an interview or do a show. And I suppose that's how I felt when I talked with Ralph. The interview itself took a back seat to just wanting a glimpse of this fellow's heart and soul. And he gave it to me. Quite a special glimpse.

I saw the pain he still feels over what he considers to be past failure in his life. I saw the grief he knows over losing Tammy and Conway. I had a peek at the tremendous admiration he has for Dolly Parton, George Strait, and so many others. And I saw the deep and appreciative love he has for his wife, Joy. But beyond all that I detected an uneasiness in a man who wonders if his life matters... Beyond that absence of arrogance, beyond the humility, beyond the desire to know and serve others so well, I detected still unasked questions that perhaps only eternity can answer.

His book, however, offers far more answers than questions. He tells us about Alan Jackson, Travis Tritt, Faron Young, Chet Atkins, Brooks and Dunn, Loretta, Conway, and Patsy. He tells the stories well of these legends of our time. Check out the book, but if you really want a treat, check out his Atlanta signing on December 4, and meet the author himself. Ralph Emery may ultimately turn out to be THE country music legend of this century. Only time will tell.

Losing Lindsey at Christmas – December 1998
Sometimes, life hurts too much. And often, when it reminds us just how short it can be is the time life hurts the most.

Earlier this month, a young mother was driving her six year old daughter, Lindsey, to a PTA meeting. Lindsey, buckled up securely in the back seat, was excited because she knew she was going to receive an award. She was to be honored for top sales in a money raising campaign for her school.

Another young woman was driving along the same highway when a tire blew out and she lost control of her car. A head on collision occurred with the car in which Lindsey was riding. The impact broke little Lindsey's neck. Brain death was almost immediate. Emergency personnel responded promptly. All the proper measures were taken to no avail.

The next day, the young mother, bruised and broken, stood by her husband at their little girl's bedside. They sobbed uncontrollably as life support equipment was disconnected.

The tears still flow. I am sure they will for a long time – perhaps forever. It is so wrong. So backwards for a child to go first. So impossible to explain to a younger sibling. It hurts too much. And all this, just before Christmas.

Is it only in the south? Is it just in my family? Or does everybody tend to measure life by the holidays? Think about the number of times you have heard someone say, "This is my x number of Christmases without him or her."

Christmas is special. Even with the overwhelming amount of commercialism to which we have all succumbed to some degree or another, Christmas is still special. Somehow, we remember that Christmas is about love. We are happy to be reminded that God is love and the greatest gift ever given was when He gave His Son, Jesus, to live and die for all mankind.

A favorite Scripture passage of mine is found in the fourth chapter of First John. It reads like this in the New American Standard version of the Bible: "Beloved, let us love one another, for love is from God; and everyone who loves is born of God and knows God. The one who does not love does not know God, for God is love. By this the love of God was manifested in us, that God has sent His only begotten Son into the world so that we might live through Him."

Live and love...

Perhaps that is why Christmas means so much to me and my family – why we measure our lives around the holiday, why we come together and forget our differences and embrace all that is good. Yes, it can be done. We can embrace all that is good in another without condoning what is blatantly bad. It may not be easy, but it is possible at Christmas.

Why? Perhaps it is because we are reminded of all our own imperfections compared to the perfection of the little baby born in that stable so long ago. The baby who would become the unblemished lamb slain for the sins of the world. The baby whose Father would grieve, whose very heart would break as He watched His Son die for you and me.

I cannot pretend to feel what Lindsey's mom feels this day, but I know Someone who can, and does. Even as He welcomes the little one into Heaven's fold, His heart aches for the mother and father whose loss He knows well.

How do I know this? How do I know that God hurts when His children hurt?

By faith, I suppose. I sometimes try to explain my beliefs, and how they have become mine. I often wonder, in this day of computer technology and cloning and trips into space, why people still do not believe. Some day, I will delve into so many areas that I feel leave no room for disbelief in this age in which we live. But, today is not the day for such delving.

Today, my heart aches for Lindsey's family because of the immeasurable pain they must feel, pain that will only be compounded when her gifts remain unopened on Christmas Day. Can anything good come out of such a heartbreaking story?

Ah, yes, if you love someone, tell them today. If you care about another, show it today. If you would do some thing, great or small, to make this a better world, do it today. We may not have another Christmas with our family or friends. Indeed, we may only have today. Live it well.

There Is Tomorrow

There is tomorrow. Oh, yes!
There is a tomorrow.
Though sometimes, when loved ones are gone
and death seems to have had the final say
we are left to wonder how we can go on this way
day after day
with only the memories of laughter
and of children at play
to haunt the empty rooms of the lives
we're tempted to feel might have been wasted
...ever mindful of the joy it seems we barely
tasted when there was only yesterday.
And we wonder if she left all cares behind
or if she shares the pain of the void created by her leaving
or if grieving is a thing unknown in the world
to which she has gone.
And, too, we wonder anew
as the past unfolds once more
why it was she who had to go before us, and not we,
why we could not be there to take her hand
and lead the way as we had done so many times
along the path of yesteryear.
And as a tear freely flows, it is as though He personally
knows the lonely anguish of each and every room.
Then as we feel Him draw near,
we can hear again the echo of the empty tomb
as the gentle promise of all the ages permits
the time-honored message of peace and everlasting hope
to permeate the places of our deepest pain
and sorrow
so that we may know there is tomorrow.

Indeed! There is a tomorrow!

One Town, One Job, One with Those Served – August 2000

I stopped by Belks on my way out of town. As I was paying for my purchase, I asked the clerk if she read the local paper.

"Oh, sure," she said, "as often as I can. I like to read it from cover to cover, but I don't always have time to do that anymore. I especially like the Sunday paper though. I have more time then, and they are putting a lot of good stuff into it now, even a magazine."

She told me a little about her favorite column. It had been written by the man I had just been talking to for a couple of hours, the managing editor.

He had told me that the publisher had pulled his column when he announced he was running for the office of coroner. Something about a conflict of interest. I reckon if an undertaker ran for that same office he would be expected not to participate in any funerals during the campaign period. Or what if a paramedic sought the position?

All I know is that lady at Belk's really did miss her favorite column. She made me want to go back to the newsroom and ask for past issues so I could read what this man had been saying over the years.

Thirty-nine years. That's how long he's been with the local paper. Started out selling classified advertising. Did a little bit of everything before he finally became managing editor. Of course, he says it's just a title now under the new management. Things change.

Things do change, don't they? And there are always those who argue that it's for the best. I wonder.

The editor and I had shared lunch at a little café in the heart of the city. It was across the road from a most interesting old building with a strange sculpture in the front yard. He told me the building had once been the newspaper office. And, before that, it had been the county jail.

I commented that it looked like an old church. Pointing to the tall steeple, I asked why anybody would convert a church to a jail.

"That was the gallows," was his response.

More than one prayer probably escaped the lips of those hung there, but I suppose that was probably the only way the old building really could ever have been compared to a church. What do I know?

My new found friend, the editor, however, knows everybody. I do mean everybody. And by first names. All ages. All colors. All makes of vehicles. Everybody spoke to him, and their faces lit up when they did. Like they were talking to an old friend.

An hour or two didn't begin to cut it. You cannot imagine how I wanted to hear this man's stories. Thirty-nine years. One town. One job. One with those he served.

Don't know what will happen after the election. Win or lose, I hope the paper will print his column again. I left his town hoping he wins. As coroner, he can continue to serve his county.

He will be retiring from the newspaper next February. Of course, he has plans to do some volunteer work with Special Olympics, and travel a bit. I cannot imagine him not being in his chair in the newsroom, and I just met him. I can only begin to imagine the loss the town will know when he is no longer there.

But, things do change. People grow older. And some day they die. And when they do, they get eulogized to some extent. Some folks even get a monument, or a statue of sorts, in a public place. And folks walk up to the piece of marble, or metal, and wonder for a brief minute or two what his or her secret was.

I was afforded two short hours, and I knew in half that time there was no "secret" to his success. Clearly, it's his dedication. He loves his town, his county, his state, and its people. He counts it a privilege to serve. Such service, from the heart! And total dedication... February will come too soon.

Single Parenthood – September 2000
His name is Tim. I just met him this week and he's a single parent raising two girls alone. I liked him.

His mom was a single parent as well. Raised him alone. He never knew his real dad. She did a good job. No doubt about it, she did a real good job.

He was in my home for several hours repairing my Macintosh G3 computer. Again. He wasn't here again. I just met him. The Mac was down again. Tim was here for close to four hours. Actually, I lost track of time. But it was plenty long enough for me to know I hope I see this kid again.

I invited him to bring his girls down on Sunday for dinner (lunch, that is). We will confirm it later. He lives on Lake Lanier so he likes to enjoy the lake whenever the weather permits. Sounds like his girls take to the water like fish, as well. No problem, I assured him my home is open year round.

You'd be surprised what you can learn about a person when you are still and alone with that person for four hours with no interruptions. My phone only rung once while he was here. A shock. I have three lines and only one of them rung one time. Unheard of.

Tim was so much like my younger son that I really was shocked at times. I thought no one in the world could be like Derrick. That's a compliment, not a cut! In case he reads this which he never does, I'm just covering my bases.

I'm talking about Tim because I want to tell you about his Friday nights. It's movie night. He and the girls, five and eight years old, rent movies and eat junk and stay awake until all hours. The youngest gives it up around 11 p.m.; the oldest can easily make it until 3 a.m.

Tim's mom, who lives nearby, gets onto him for such behavior. The girls need their rest, she says. Saturday is ballet day. They need lots of energy to dance and they have to concentrate as well.

Me? I hope he never stops doing Friday nights. I figure, however, that he may have two, possibly three more good years left with the oldest. By then she will be doing her own thing with her own friends. They start earlier and earlier trying to wean themselves from their parents these days.

If Tim's lucky and I'm banking on him, they just might save a Friday night a month for him when they are older. I hope they will. In a matter of hours, I could see how special he is. Surely his kids know.

But I didn't. I didn't know or acknowledge how special my dad was until after he was gone. He worked three jobs to support his seven kids. My mom never worked outside the home. So time was limited with Daddy. As I look back, I realize it was from Daddy that I learned to entertain, to talk, to "live." He enjoyed life and his enthusiasm for the human experience was so contagious that all those around him were infected by it. In fact, I saw my cousin, Joyce, last weekend. I hadn't seen her in 30 years. We visited for about four hours and had a ball – talked, laughed, reminisced. She said I brought back memories of how Uncle Alton's and Aunt Mary's family always enjoyed life. It is good to be reminded.

There's so much we take for granted. Tim and I talked about how he plays with his kids, how much he loves them. He told me how the little one, at three years old, jumped over board into the lake one summer. Didn't fall, mind you. She jumped. He did, too. Instantly. What's 30 knots or standing still to a toddler? She hasn't done it again. His heart couldn't take it.

I was so thrilled to meet this young man and hear him talk about his kids. And the dad he never knew. It was cool to observe no bitterness. Even at his young age, I think he already knows life is too short to pepper it with bitterness and resentment.

I'm looking forward to introducing him to my son. Derrick hasn't been married and does not have kids, but otherwise the similarities were uncanny. Maybe the two of them could put together a seminar on how to enjoy life and the rest of us could take a few hours out of our far too busy days to attend. Four hours is plenty of time to catch the enthusiasm. What you do with it once you catch it, now that's up to you. I never thanked my dad for the best gift he ever gave me. I wish I had.

A Piece of History – October 2000

I've never been attracted to much of anything that could be perceived as scary. I've only seen one Stephen King movie, and have never read any of his books. If I'm flipping channels and hear the music (you know the kind of music I'm talking about), I quickly move on to another channel. Scary just doesn't cut it with me.

Yet, Halloween was always the favorite holiday for both my sons when they were growing up. I never knew if it was the candy, the dress up routine, or just all the mischief they thought they were entitled to get into when Halloween came. But they loved it.

And ghost stories? I suppose I always figured I had no choice but to let them have their place. I just didn't know how important that place was until I met the professor, Dr. William Lynwood Montell, that is. I met him in mid-September when he was in Atlanta to promote his latest book, "Ghosts Across Kentucky."

I had to know immediately if he had ever actually seen a ghost. Just one, he said, when he was six years old. And one other time as an adult, every hair on his body had stood on edge, but he only had sensed the ghostly presence that time, he didn't see it.

This utterly delightful gentleman of the south, who has made storytelling his life, taught at Western Kentucky University for many years, but is "retired" now. Actually, he is presently researching and writing four more books, and is the most-ever requested statewide speaker for the Kentucky Humanities Council (KHC). This year, his presentations are called "Ghost Stories from Across Kentucky," and "Stories As Generational Bonding Agents." He has authored more than 15 books to date on folklore, several of which are devoted to the telling of ghost stories!

When asked what folklore is, he says it is the study of the 99.99 per cent of the world's population whose names are never included in history books. For that reason, he's not interested in writing books about kings, queens, presidents, or governors.

So what prompted this professor to write books about ghosts? He began actively collecting death premonition accounts and ghost stories while teaching at Campbellsville College, Campbellsville,

Kentucky, from 1963-69. With the assistance of hundreds of students over the years he has compiled many of these supernatural accounts for publication. The first of four books to date was "Ghosts Along The Cumberland: Deathlore in the Kentucky Foothills" (1975). This book has been reprinted three times in cloth and three times in paperback. The clothback edition is now out of print. The latest collection is in "Ghosts Across Kentucky." Coming next year will be "Kentucky Family and House Ghosts."

So what has my encounter with the professor taught me? According to Dr. Montell, "Supernatural stories are rich in historical detail about houses and related buildings, and provide details relevant to people's believed-to-be-true encounters with the supernatural. Some stories go back to pioneer times, while others are tied to ante-bellum homes and family progenitors who were present at that time. Some even reflect the bitterness of slavery conditions and fratricidal conflict during the Civil War."

He adds, "Ghost stories contain a lot of historical content in that they describe folk practices and beliefs that have long been forgotten except by older residents. It is important to record and place these stories in print so that the historical and personal information contained in them will be preserved for future generations yet to come."

Who would ever have thought that ghost stories had historical value? If you are in doubt at this point, try to remember a story or two that you have heard. Let yourself recall them in vivid detail. For instance, Mary Ella was my grandmother's oldest child who died at age four, and my grandmother used to give me icicle skin talking about her encounters with the dead girl. Right now, as I type these words, I can still envision the youngster standing by the fence gate at the northwest corner of the yard, the one leading up to the house from the barn, just standing there longing to cross the line and come back.

Learning To Keep My Mouth Shut – November 2000
If you want to know what's going on in town, what politician can be trusted and which one or ones cannot, who's done what to whom and why, then find the spot (usually some kind of eatery) where the men congregate on Any Town Square, USA and listen. Just listen. You will blow every thing if you ask questions, because the locals will then ask ten questions to your one.

I was traveling back from Albany last week and stopped off in Thomaston for lunch. Earlier, I had stopped in Butler at the town restaurant, a weathered old house with a wrap around porch about a block off the square. It smelled good as soon as I opened my car door, but the vittles there would have made my gut angry for days. We're talking ham and cabbage, sweet potatoes, and big white limas all at one meal. My husband would have been in dietary heaven. Me? I'm not tough enough to eat like that.

So I bought a glass of iced tea and a cassette tape. Oh, yeah, the local restaurant was run by a cute young woman wearing hunting fatigues, black lace up boots, and a t-shirt. She was interesting and grew more so when I noticed that the pretty girl on the cassette tape by the cash register resembled her. I asked. The same. I bought her tape. She said she had made the recording in 1999.

I drove away to a Loretta Lynn, Tammy Wynette, Patsy Cline blend with a touch of something a little different. Don't know what to call it yet, but I know I'm hearing the same sound from some of the new singing stars that are calling themselves country. Oh well, time goes by and things change.

Except in Thomaston. Well, actually, I suppose things are changing there, too, since the pool table is gone. I was shocked to find I had two eatery choices that were located on the square. I thought that was a bit unusual. You are lucky these days to find even one restaurant still located on an old town square. I chose English's Café on the southwest corner and walked in to a rectangular shaped serving arena at the front of the store. The L-shaped windows of the building gave the owner and anybody who chose to sit on the bar stools, which were available on three sides of the service area, full view of the town square.

It was early, not even noon yet, and I was the first one there. There was a sign just inside the door announcing that chicken salad was the daily special. I ordered a chicken salad sandwich, chips and tea. I received change back out of a five. Nice. The sandwich was good, too.

Before anybody else showed up, I asked about the big metal box sitting in the center of the area where Diane, the owner, stood. It's our bun warmer, she said. Biggest bun warmer I'd ever seen. And then the people started coming.

The first fellow walked in and never said a word. One hot dog coming up, said Diane, and he just nodded. When they others started drifting in, one ordered the chicken salad sandwich. Another ordered two hot dogs. The rest? They all ordered a hamburger, the house special.

It was the darndest hamburger I'd ever seen. Diane reached into the big bun warmer, pulled out a bun, opened it and spooned scrambled hamburger meat on top, then squeezed some kind of special sauce (catchup based) over the meat, put the top on it, and handed it to one eager diner after another.

After about the third order I blew it. Once the locals started coming in, I knew to sit there, be quiet, mind my own business, and just listen. Yep, I knew better, but I had to ask about that burger preparation.

"You must not be from around here?" echoed the voices around the counter as all eyes suddenly turned on me. I admitted I lived just 25 miles away, but quickly added I'd been living there less than three years. Nobody was impressed with my pathetic excuse for ignorance.

I learned that the English Café burger had been prepared that way since 1929. When the pool table was still there a player could turn from the table to order a burger, have it served up, and never miss a shot. I believe it. We're talking seconds here.

I'll go back. I'll order that burger next time, keep my mouth shut, and listen. The stories were just getting good before I had to up and blew it!

Terry Kay's "Voice Like God's" – August 2001

I met him the year "White Dog" was published. I walked right smack dab into him at the foot of the escalator at the Hyatt Regency in Atlanta. I was at a Southeastern Bookseller's Association convention and he was there too, but he wasn't wearing a name tag, so I didn't even know he was an author.

The first words I ever heard him say were "Excuse me" although I'm sure I was the one who walked into him. And he said it in that unforgettable voice that Jim Minter has referred to as "a voice like God's."

Certainly, Terry Kay's spoken and written voice is unforgettable, as is his warmth and talent. A newspaperman from way back, Terry turned novelist somewhere along the line. I'm not sure anybody knows just when the transition took place. But everybody knows success, as the world tends to define it, found him the year "To Dance with the White Dog" came out.

That would have been 1990, I believe, when Peachtree Publishers, in Atlanta, first brought it out in hard cover. Soon afterwards it was made into a Hallmark Hall of Fame movie and the whole country got to dance with the delightful white dog who made his way from Terry's pen into our hearts.

Jump forward a decade... I was having coffee earlier this year with Terry, at a book store in Athens, when we both observed a lady beside us who was going through a huge stack of "angel" books. I, of course, had to ask about her interest. She said she was looking for the right book for a friend whose mom had just died.

Terry immediately recommended "To Dance with the White Dog." I was irritated that I did not think to recommend it first. Actually, I believe that was the first time I realized just how timeless the book is.

Now get this... Terry recently received a phone call of which most writers only dream. He learned, eleven years after it was first published, that "To Dance with the White Dog" has become a hit on the other side of the world! It had been published a while back by the Shinchosha Publishing Company in Japan. But it wasn't really "discovered" until early this year when an assistant book store manager read it, wrote a blurb about it and shared his impressions with the store manager.

They set up a small display in the back of the store and sold 187 copies in the month of April alone. They moved the display to the front of the store and sold 471 copies in May.

Enter the sales person for the publishing company. She convinces the publisher to use what the assistant store manager wrote in a national campaign. Immediately Shinchosha printed 12,000 more copies. Later, in June, they printed 20,000 more copies. In early July, another 20,000 were printed. Then on July 23, 50,000 more came off the press.

At this time, more than 500,000 are in print, but who's counting? Those of us who know and love Terry are just rejoicing that this warm southern gentleman, who also happens to be a genre jumping genius, is being discovered beyond our own turf. His latest novel, "Taking Lottie Home," is among several works that continually attest to his talent. Other novels include "Shadow Song," "The Kidnapping of Aaron Greene," "The Runaway," "Dark Thirty," "After Eli," and "The Year the Lights Came On."

"To Dance with the White Dog" based on the life and experience of Terry's father may just be taking off in Japan, but it still remains alive and well in the United States. I suspect I am among many who rejoice with this native Georgian over the timeless success of his work and the awesome way he represents his home state through both his published works and his life.

Paul Grice, Teacher – October 2001

Back in 1986, when I resigned from my job as a nurse at a family practice office where I had worked for five years, my older son was elated. "Great," was his response, "now you can chaperone our FFA camping trip."

I had not heard about that trip prior to making my announcement about resigning. I often wonder now how much I missed during those years when I was so sure my kids were old enough that they didn't really need me to be around all the time.

But we won't go there today. There is something else I want to talk about. Or somebody else.

That somebody would be Paul Grice. It was he and I who took seventeen boys and three girls to North Georgia that fall for the annual FFA camping trip. It was the adventure of a lifetime for me and my first real glimpse into the life of this dedicated teacher.

On this trip, however, I only began to get to know the man his kids affectionately called just plain "Grice." Over the years I learned more about this wise and insightful teacher.

Paul Grice knew how to let kids be kids. Warts and all. He knew that growing up was hard and nobody had all the answers yet, that each child was unique, and that where we as parents and teachers failed them, nature would not.

So he taught his kids – and there were thousands of them over the years – he taught them how to live, how to work with their hands, how to survive and thrive. There was never any question about how you could use what Paul Grice taught you "out in the real world."

He taught his kids to love and appreciate nature and be alert to all the lessons it would continuously teach them. Somebody else did that too. A long time ago. About 2000 years, in fact. Much of the truth taught by Jesus Christ was in parables, and many of the truths hidden therein revolved around nature and the creation.

Another Paul, of New Testament fame, took the teachings of Christ even further when, in his letter to the church at Rome, he made it clear that the ungodly and the unbelievers were without excuse when it came to recognizing God, "For since the creation of the world, God's invisible attributes, His eternal power and divine nature, have been clearly seen, being understood through what has been made."

The Paul who penned those words, as well as the Paul I remember today, would caution us once more I'm sure – even as beautiful as is the creation – to look beyond it to the Creator for comfort, courage, wisdom, guidance and eternal life. By the way, that Paul also knew how to get down on the same level with those he longed to teach.

For anyone reading these words, who may be worried about the present state of world affairs, who is unsure of what tomorrow holds, who may be floundering or fearful, I want to pass on one sustaining truth, a truth that Paul Grice sought to convey, as well. It is this: somebody loves you just like you are, will meet you right where you are, and will work with you to become what you want and need to be, not just for today, but for all eternity.

Grice taught his kids that when he shared with them his love for nature. Perhaps he did so because he knew he'd be gone one day and he wanted to leave his kids the tools they would need to keep on learning.

Paul Grice didn't just tell you to touch a leaf or smell a flower. He showed you how do it, and encouraged you to do it often and well. And he taught kids how to climb trees and mountains, both literally and figuratively.

He made it clear if you didn't get it right the first time that you must keep on trying. No, he didn't just teach his kids how to keep climbing, he showed them right up until what too many perceive as the end. In truth, the brain tumor was just his door to the other side where I'm sure adventure beyond compare was waiting.

Today, I invite you to remember those teachers, mentors or shining lights in your life who have helped to teach you how to live. Not to just exist, but to really live! Perhaps many of them have also crossed over to the other side. As you recall their influence, try to imagine what folks will think about you one day when you have gone on.

There's still time for you to influence those future thoughts. Even if you don't think you owe it to the Paul Grices of the world who dedicate their lives to helping you learn how to live successfully, you owe it to yourself.

Strangers Sharing Lunch – November 2001
We learned that her name was Eliza. She called him Dan. That's how they introduced themselves when they accepted my invitation to join us at our table for lunch at the Concord Café on Sunday.

Oddly enough, I did not get my usual look from my Dan when I issued the invitation. I am beginning to think after all these years that I finally have him trained. It appears he has now realized a stranger is just a friend you don't know yet.

When we left the restaurant he actually commented on how much he enjoyed the couple and how beautiful she was. Of course, he never bothered to remember aloud that she was wearing a suit the same color as the one I had on the night I met him some 35 years ago.

Oh, well, if the years teach us anything they teach us how to forgive. At least it was clear that he still liked the personality behind that brilliant rose red color.

She had stopped at our table as they entered the restaurant to speak to my hubby. She, a total stranger, tall, thin and graceful, was so forward as to suggest that he go fix himself another plate and let her have the one which he had just set before himself.

My, how I was enjoying that encounter! I wondered if she and I were kin.

I recalled a time some years back when the physician I worked for had taken the office staff out for lunch. As we walked into the restaurant, and by this booth of four strange men, I stopped to inquire about a platter of something on their table that I did not recognize. They offered me a taste. I tasted. To this day, the folks with whom I am still in contact from that office call me a floozie.

By the way, just try nonchalantly, unless you want to be labeled a floozie, to glance at the plates of other diners as you enter a restaurant. That is the best way by far to choose what you'd like to have. In fact, if you ask to be seated near the back of the establishment you will have an opportunity to view more selections as you meander slowly to your table. Decide what you like and when you server comes, tell him to forget the menu and discreetly point to the person eating what you want, ask what they are having, and order it.

Back to Concord and Eliza and Dan. We learned they had been on their way from Atlanta to someplace in Wyoming on September 11. Eliza talked about how brilliant Dan is and how he knows maps and all sorts of things. He had been watching when they crossed the Mississippi and suddenly turned northward.

He whispered to her that the pilot had just changed course. She had not noticed, but she knew her man and never for a second doubted that he knew what he was talking about, so she wondered why the pilot had taken such action.

Within seconds the voice they will never forget came through the air. "This is your captain," he said, "and this is not a joke. I am serious. We have just been ordered to land in Little Rock. American Airlines is under attack. Two of our planes have just crashed into the World Trade Centers."

The couple said cell phones began to literally fly out of hand bags, brief cases and carry on luggage. They said folks started dialing contacts down below for confirmation. For details. For more information.

Once they reached Little Rock they had to circle for more than 30 minutes while waiting for their turn to land. At first there was chaos. Then, in a matter of hours, everything became eerily quiet.

They inquired about car rentals and bus travel. It took two and half days to get a car which they and the couple accompanying them drove back to Atlanta. They said retrieving their car from Hartsfield International Airport in Atlanta proved to be yet another adventure.

Then suddenly I realized why I could not help but invite these two "strangers" to join Daniel and me for lunch. Not one negative thing had they said about their entire adventure of September 11. In fact, in the hour or so we shared together, not one negative thing did they say about anything or anyone. In spite of great sadness, some fear and much inconvenience it was clear that this delightful couple had turned their 9/11 experience into a special memory.

As they shared their memories with two strangers, I thought *life just doesn't get better*, and the food was good, too, as usual!

Customer Service – August 2003

As you know there's not much I don't think my hubby can do. He is the ultimate yard man and repair person. He can build just about anything I can persuade him that I need. He can even take a jet engine apart and put it back together. He truly is amazing.

EXCEPT -- I bet you knew there was about to be an "except," didn't you?

I'm beginning to think he is actually afraid of computers. Never thought there would be a day when I would think, much less audibly say or actually write the words, that he is afraid of anything mechanical.

When it comes to computers, he does not even like to be in the same room with one. If I want him to read something on the screen before me, I know I have to print it out. Yep, waste another tree. I think he figures if it's not on paper then it was not meant for him to read it.

Except at work, of course – he assures me that he reads all correspondence at work. Hates it, but does it. Accepts the fact that it is necessary in his workplace. But there is no convincing him it's necessary in his homeplace.

So after two years of continuous problems with a computer that had to have been put together and programmed by somebody with a Monday morning hangover or worse, I gave up on a Sunday evening about three weeks ago and drove up to Office Depot in Fayetteville about an hour before they closed.

I guessed that the manager must have spotted me when I walked through the door, and that he had come to recognize the look that must have been on my face.

I had absolutely had it with the piece of junk I had struggled with for 24 months. It actually is the first bad, as in truly evil, computer I have ever owned. To date, I have outgrown several and have come to know a smooth running sweetie when I sit down before one.

So the manager himself, Jeff Key, listens to my woes and my needs. In a matter of minutes, he custom built an order for me (on paper). The price was awesome. He assured me it was exactly what I needed.

I waited 18 days for delivery. The old computer practically bit the dust last week, two days before the new one arrived.

The new system came. It is perfect and I got it at a perfect price. I am elated.

I left there thinking of how close I had come to giving up on Office Depot about two years earlier. I had repeatedly gone in that same store and had repeatedly been met with somewhere between poor and no service for several months (a first ever for that chain). I since have shopped around at a Staples or Office Max here and there, even bought a few things from Wal-Mart. I have no complaint about the other stores, but I missed the convenience of the Office Depot store layout/design as well as the product choices, so I am glad to be back with them.

Isn't it awesome when you occasionally discover true service in today's workplace? Real, honest to goodness customer service with folks who listen to what you say, seek to understand your needs, and strive to meet those needs in a timely fashion can't be beat! Jeff Key was right. The new system is exactly what I needed. Just like I knew that last piece of equipment was a lemon from the get-go, I know this baby will serve me well. How foolish we are to think one person cannot make a difference. With one order, one genuine act of customer service, this store manager has erased my former frustrations with Office Depot and brought me back into the fold.

As I write this, I am reminded of a sales associate at the Rich's Store in Columbus, Georgia, who almost single handedly made me a loyal Rich's shopper again last year. There again, frustrations at another store with other associates had driven me away. I love to shop at Rich's and I am glad to have been drawn back to the chain.

There just are no words to describe how valuable client centered service is in any workplace setting, but, because I am so extraordinarily thankful to be sitting at the keyboard of a quality piece of equipment this morning, I just had to try!

An Italian Influence – October 2003

I've wanted to go to Italy since my late teens. And I suppose there have been a few occasions when I could have visited the country. Yet, somehow, I always talk myself out of going abroad with reminders that there are still places in my homeland which I have not seen. It could be that the main reason for my decision to stay in America is patriotic, or it could be that I'm scared of water.

I don't like the idea of flying for hours with nothing but billowing waves of water beneath me. I don't even like long bridges that take me out over large bodies of water. And you can be assured that a cruise has never made it to my list of things to do.

So I make do in my homeland. And I am blessed. About four years ago I discovered the best Italian café yet. Actually, my husband, Daniel, and I discovered it together. We were in Columbus, and both of us appreciate local eateries (especially those situated near the courthouse square of small southern towns!), so we asked several folks if they could recommend one.

One lady said there was a really wonderful locally owned and operated Italian café just a couple of miles from the mall where we were shopping. We made our way over to Caffe Amici's and have been loyal patrons ever since. "Cucina Dei Vecchi Tempi" (old style home cooking) is on the front of the evening menu, followed by the promise that all dishes are made to order, with only the best and freshest ingredients.

The only downside, if one would dare to call it a downside, is that one should not plan to go there for a "quick bite." It is the place for a relaxed, casual dining experience and nothing less! Even at lunch.

When I took my husband there on Tuesday of this week, for his birthday, I resolved that I had to mention the little cafe to you. Just in case you are ever in Columbus, you should look it up. Caffe Amici's. You will not regret it.

While we are talking Italian, let me also tell you about an artist I have discovered. I met Victor Gagliardi at a recent Southeastern Bookseller's Convention, where he was exhibiting some of his work. I was mesmerized. Immediately.

I tried to interview him. Now, normally nobody turns me down. Really. Folks just talk to me. Easily. And everybody likes to talk about themselves. Right?

Wrong. Victor did not want to talk about himself at all. It was quite apparent that he wants his work to speak for itself. He is wise.

"A Turning Point–Images to Words" by Victor Gagliardi features 150 pages of exceptionally inspiring photography, accompanied by remarkably well chosen inspirational quotations. Of course, many of you know I'm a collector of inspirational books and quotable quotes, so you might say I was an easy mark for his extraordinary work. My guess is you would be, too.

I'm determined that someday I will have my in-depth interview with the artist. Oh, yeah, we are talking true artist in every sense of the word. It was almost like I could sense greatness in his presence. I know we are all wonderful human beings with great potential, but this man has that special something which makes you know he is not only choosing to act on his God-given potential, but may somehow have been uniquely chosen to do the work he does.

Since purchasing "A Turning Point," I have sat down with it on several occasions in an old rocker that I enjoy in one of my upstairs bedrooms. The rocker sits in a corner by a window where the morning light streams though in a country magical kind of way. It is a good place to lose myself in Victor's book.

Keep your eyes and ears open for Victor Gagliardi. Yet another very gifted artist is among us. By the way, I did find out that his grandparents came to America around 1912. To Italy, we owe a dept of gratitude not only for wonderful culinary gifts, but for important food for the soul as well.

Fairhope, Alabama – December 2003
For five days, I have been bathed in the reflections of Fairhope. Like past visits to Montana and Maine, this visit to Fairhope will leave me changed. Change is good. Almost always. It expands one. Challenges one. Intrigues one – if one lets it.

I arrived on Sunday, and almost immediately found myself enveloped in a delightful chat with Louis Mapp. He and his wife were sitting in front of the fireplace at the foot of the spectacular Christmas tree just off the main entry hall. She was an elegant picture of beauty and grace there in the amber light of the lovely tree, and I said so to her husband. He and I then embarked on the conversation that would become my introduction to this breathtaking resort area.

It truly is a grand and fitting Christmas tree that welcomes guests to this wonderful Grand Hotel at Point Clear, just across the creek from Fairhope, Alabama. I understand the tree was actually featured in USA Today a week or so ago. Deserving it is of such attention, for sure.

Well, I said it. Alabama. And I compared it with Maine and Montana. Now, all of you know this Georgia girl knows no state can hold a candle to Georgia, and who would have thought Alabama would even be in the running. Certainly not I. Not until these past few days.

I will leave this place tomorrow with a new appreciation for this state which does not deserve what we Georgians say about it. No words can describe the love I have come to feel for this bay in only a few short days. And when I leave for home tomorrow, it will be with an even greater admiration for small towns everywhere.

Not that I don't always appreciate small towns. I do. Far more that most folks, I suspect. When I'm traveling, I like to stop and eat at local restaurants on the square of small towns all over America. There you can take the pulse of the town and quickly know the pace of its heartbeat.

It's a shame that one must quickly observe such a vital sign. It would be better by far to walk the streets. Visit shops. Frequent all local eateries. Find a way to be invited into a few homes... Ah, then one would be able to observe real life and count the individual heartbeats. Alas, I am too often left with no more than the collective pulse rate and I settle. Because I must.

But I have not had to settle this week. Louis Mapp was only the first of more than a dozen "locals" with whom I have had quality exchanges of mind, heart, and perhaps, soul. Two hours spent one morning at Over the Transom Book Store in Downtown Fairhope was assuredly a highlight. Sonny Brewer and his partners made my morning! Sonny is a writer, editor, singer and phenomenal conversationalist. He is at work presently on a novel about The Poet of Tolstoy Park. Watch for it near the end of 2004.

Certainly, the royal pink and purple sunsets mesmerize one in this location. The trees, drenched in their friendly moss, invite a melding that few places can pull off. I am happy. I am at one with this setting. It is unusual for me to feel this good so far from home. It is fitting.

There is no way to know if I will return again to Fairhope, Alabama. I seldom retrace my steps. Oh, I want to. I say that I will. I mean well. I know that many places are worthy of return visits. Yet, somehow, new and strange places keep calling to me. And I find that I choose the unknown far more often that the known.

So, as I sit here in the business center of The Grand Hotel, pecking away on this borrowed keyboard, it is with a minimally sad awareness that when I leave tomorrow I may never come this way again. And that's okay, as it is my way. But I invite you, if you ever have the opportunity to see this area, to stay at this wonderful old hotel, to sit before its fireplace, to walk the streets of its town, please do so. It would be my gift to you – the sharing of this lovely little Alabama town nestled in the embrace of its unforgettable and magical bay waters.

Evander Holyfield – March 2004

Yes, he has ten children, and yes, some of them were born out of wedlock. Yes, that would seem to indicate that his morals are not what some folks would tend to think they ought to be. Yes, he hits other men and gets hit by them, for money. I'm thinking: not exactly my kinda guy...

Oh, I've seen televised interviews in which he has handled himself very well. And yes, I've heard him say things worth hearing. My younger son, who had met him a few years back, and had some degree of interaction with him at a bowling alley they both frequented, kept telling me I ought to meet Evander – that I would like him.

Still... A fighter? An adulterer? I did not think the man was somebody I would enjoy getting to know. I was wrong!

He's real. He is downright refreshing! A sinner saved by grace, just like all the rest of us. I don't know where we all get off thinking one sin is more or less than the others. But we do it, don't we?

At least, Evander has not turned his back on his children. Not only is he raising them, loving them, caring for them, being there for them, but he still finds time to reach out to other children whose fathers and mothers have abandoned them.

He just returned from a mission trip to India. I enjoyed hearing him talk about the sparse conditions of the place where he stayed. It was not comfortable at all, but he said it was easy for him to go there and do his thing because he knew "what he would be going back home to."

And then get this... now GET it, okay? Evander equated his trip to India to being kind of like Jesus coming to Earth from Heaven. Jesus could do it, because He knew where He came from and to Whom He would be returning.

At first, his comparison took me by surprise, and I stood there thinking SILENTLY to myself "Surely you are not comparing yourself to Jesus?"

But he was. He did. He makes scripture come to life. He applies it to real life as best he can. Not that he thinks he is like Jesus, but clearly, he wants to be.

As he spoke at length to me, I was recalling words penned by the author of the Book of Hebrews: "Therefore, since we have so great a cloud of witnesses surrounding us, let us also lay aside every encumbrance, and the sin which so easily entangles us, and let us run with endurance the race that is set before us, fixing our eyes on Jesus, the author and perfecter of faith, who for the joy set before Him endured the cross, despising the shame, and has sat down at the right hand of the throne of God."

I doubt there is a Bible verse that could more appropriately describe Evander Holyfield. I'm betting this is one man who will never be so "heavenly minded that he becomes of no earthly good." Not hardly. Evander knows where he has come from and knows that "for a lack of knowledge the people perish." He knows he is still growing spiritually. He is humble. He is thankful.

I am humbled. I am thankful I have met him. Thought you might want to know: there's about to be a hundred more Holyfields! He is adopting a hundred kids in various impoverished countries all around the world. They will be given his name. Through Global Peace Initiative he will pay for their care and education. He will do his part to be sure that those hundred kids do not "perish from a lack of knowledge."

Of course, when Evander made reference to that scripture passage, he was speaking spiritually. But those words were coming from the lips of a man who grew up knowing how it felt to do/be without... Ah, but he was loved by a God-fearing mama who cherished him and gave him all he really needed, and then some!

She has gone on to be with the God that Evander now strives to serve. Though he can no longer give back to her for all she gave to him, he seeks to pass on the legacy she left him. He seeks to educate, to inspire, to actively care for a world beyond his own.

In doing so, it would appear that he is trying to give back to the God and Father of us all Who has blessed him with so much. Yeah, I like this guy -- a lot!

PART TWO – Me and Mine

Remembering One's First Love – July 1991

The death of one's first love can drive home the reality of mortality very quickly.

I was only eleven. My sister was six years old and our friend was eight. It was the year of Bonanza. It was the year that Hoss, Adam and Little Joe came into our hearts.

For the first few months, whenever we played "Bonanza," out in the fields and woods around our house, we always argued over who would have whom as a boyfriend, mate, lover or whatever it is six, eight and eleven year old girls expect from a make believe male friend.

Except Adam, Hoss and Little Joe were not make believe! They came into our homes each week by way of television and deeper into our hearts with each episode.

It took a few months of discussing, arguing and pouting before I finally got my way. I wanted Little Joe, but it was repeatedly proposed that I should have Adam since I was the oldest of the three starstruck females. So, the only fair thing to do was, of course, take turns.

Swapping boyfriends went on for a number of weeks. I don't recall ever marrying Hoss, but I alternated between Adam and Little Joe quite often until the day came that I could stand it no longer.

Little Joe had won my heart. I could not betray him with any more involvement with his brothers. Besides, seniority had to count for something. So, as the oldest, I finally demanded Little Joe all for myself. Either I got him or I just wouldn't play.

After that, when we played together, I got him. I did learn years later that Lynda and Veronica continued to share him when I was not around. As a matter of fact I don't think they ever quite so enthusiastically insisted that I play with them, in that world of fantasy we had created together, after the day I delivered my ultimatum.

I wonder how many other women, whose little girl hearts were stolen by the good looking young cowboy nearly thirty years ago, grieved with me this week at the death of Michael Landon.

I am sure we all thought that if anyone could beat the odds he could. But he couldn't, and he didn't, and we are all reminded again of the certainty of death. I liked the courage Landon exhibited in the interviews where he so readily discussed his illness, his chances of getting well, and the possibility of not regaining his health.

I like the way he said that if he did not beat the cancer, and continue his adventures here on earth, then yet another adventure still lay ahead.

No wonder I loved him so. For many years I have thought of death as an adventure, life's greatest adventure, perhaps.

So, today, I recall the most renowned adventurer of all the ages. No adventurer who ever left his home to traverse unknown and unfamiliar territories has made a greater impact in life than did Jesus Christ when he journeyed to earth.

Why?

Because He left Heaven to come to earth. And He came to explore and claim the heart of man. What an adventure that must have been! What a mission! What a calling!.

I am sure His own heart must have broken a thousand times as He made His way through the territories He came to claim. But His was a successful journey because my heart belongs to Him today. Now, nearly 2000 years after he came to stake His claim on our unclaimed hearts, I suspect I am only one of millions who is glad He was willing to set out on that greatest adventure in all of history. I am glad He left Heaven to come to earth and make the way for me to one day leave earth and go back to heaven.

I 'm glad, too, that Little Joe was my first love and I am thankful for his influence in my life and in the lives of so many others. I'm glad the years taught me to share him gracefully as Bonanza proved to be only the beginning, for with Little House on the Prairie and Highway to Heaven he continued to endear himself to us.

With both his life and his death I'm glad Little Joe touched my life. I'm glad to have been reminded yet again of the adventure which awaits me because of Jesus Christ's willingness to embark on that adventure of all the ages so many years ago. I'm glad that Little Joe and others have come into my heart over the years, but I'm super glad that only Jesus has been able and capable of staking permanent claim.

The Drill Sergeant's Run – August 1991
"Wear your gym clothes and meet me out in front of the barracks in the morning at 0700 hours."

With those words the drill sergeant went one way and the young man went another for the evening.

At their morning rendezvous the young private was instructed to set his own pace for the three mile run, but to sprint each hill. The drill sergeant stayed in step all along the way as they discussed the private's behavior the night before.

There had been no altercation in the E club, but less than twelve hours earlier the young man had let it be known that he was quite willing to fight for a place to sit down in the crowded establishment. The older and wiser gentleman had not felt like that was a good enough reason to come to blows with a fellow soldier who had not wanted company at his table.

The private had not known he was being observed. He learned, however, that drill sergeants are everywhere. You don't always see them, hear them, or sense their presence, but their ability to know everything that goes on with their charges is unsurpassed. Even mothers can't hold a candle to them!

And that morning as the sun rose over San Antonio he learned something else about drill sergeants. They cared.

They cared about their trainees. They cared enough, not just to run them, but to run with them. They cared enough, not to talk at them, but to talk with them. They cared enough, not only to do their jobs well, but to do their jobs with a compassion and sincerity which left the young private knowing that the United States Army cared about him. Not just about his attitude, or his appearance, or his training, but the whole of him. He was cared about as a person.

A year later he was telling the story about the drill sergeant's subtle and wisely chosen disciplinary action and he was telling it as though it was a fond memory. Perhaps, it is a story he will tell for many years.

The 1991 Class Reunion – August 1991

Seldom in life does a long anticipated event turn out to be every bit as wonderful and exciting as one expects. But my 25 year high school class reunion was such an occasion.

The conversation and the laughter and the hugs and the music and the food and the balloons – even the rain and the sunshine – have found their niche in the special memory bank I keep tucked away in a corner of my heart. In fact, I don't think it ever gets any better than the 36 plus hours I spent with so many friends in Albany, GA last weekend. We were the Mitchell County High Class of '66, but Camilla offered no place for us to gather this year so some of the gang chose the perfect spot in Albany.

It all started on Friday evening, at 7 p.m., with cocktails and hors d'oeuvres in the Colonial Room at Merry Acres Hotel. Even the hotel was ideal. The rooms were spacious, clean and comfortable, even a bit luxurious, with beautifully manicured grounds.

I think, perhaps, it was the hotel itself which set the stage for me to have a really neat weekend. One of my old apartments in Albany has been turned into an attorney's office; the other one has been torn down, reminding me that the years bring change and change takes its toll. But the Merry Acres Hotel, which has been in Albany as long as I can remember, is still standing and seems to be growing better with the years.

Once you hit forty, you begin to truly appreciate, from the heart, anything which seems to be getting better with the years!

I also attended my 10, 15 and 20 year class reunions. Now, after the 25th I can readily say the get-togethers just keep getting better each time. Since "why?" is, and always has been, one of my favorite words, naturally, I ask myself why the reunions keep getting better.

Proving that just about anybody can exhibit some degree of insight some of the time, the Russian/American writer, Ayn Rand once wrote *"love and friendship are profoundly personal, selfish values... an expression of self-esteem, a response to one's own values in the person of another."*

Perhaps she hit on the reason I have found my reunions so personally rewarding. Each time we have all gotten together (always there's been at least half out of a class of nearly 92 to show up for these gatherings), my sense of self has been renewed. I'm not endowed with an over-abundance of self-esteem, but what I have emanates from the realization that God loves me – no matter what! And I suppose that is how I feel when I'm with friends from years past. They, too, seem to love me, no matter what.

There is great wealth and immeasurable strength and courage to be found in such realization. When we know we are loved, when a true sense of belonging reigns in our hearts, life is worth living!

Knowing that there is somebody somewhere who will pull for and with you when you struggle, who will literally help to pull you up again when you feel like you're failing, who will be proud of you when you succeed, who will be there to share the good times and the bad, and hold to the memories of both with equal respect – aware that such inconsistency and uncertainty is the stuff of which life is made – makes all the difference in the world between living, really living, and just existing...

No greater happiness can be had than that which comes with knowing that there are those whose love for you is like your love for yourself. For, in a powerful and unique way, you are them and they are you.

Emerson said it well with these words, *"The glory of friendship is not the outstretched hand, nor the kindly smile, not the joy of companionship; it is the spiritual inspiration that comes to one when he discovers that someone believes in him and is willing to trust him with his friendship."*

People Watching – November 1992
It was the only empty chair in the entire eating arena. There were no empty tables. He was sitting with his back to the table, and to the empty chair on the other side of it, which my tired back and legs wanted to fill.

So, I bought my Chick-fil-A sandwich and lemonade and walked over to ask if the chair was taken or if he was saving it for someone.

Oh, no, ma'am, he said, as he turned his chair around and welcomed me into his space. For a brief instant I was sorry he had turned around because I knew he had been watching the people move through the mall, carrying their packages in their arms and their life's stories on their faces.

It is one of my favorite pastimes, too. Watching people. So, I felt bad about interrupting him, especially if he doesn't get to do it any more often than I do.

I felt sorry for only an instant, however, because, for the next forty minutes or so, the 86 year old gentleman in the crisply starched and ironed khaki shirt and trousers with nary a tooth in his mouth, shared himself with me. He shared from a heart of joy which evidenced a deep appreciation for life and America and all the blessings which have been his.

"Mama," his wife of more than 60 years, was at home in Fort Valley. He was at the mall with his daughter. He had come along for the ride, and while she did some early Christmas shopping, he was watching the people.

He and "Mama" had retired in 1972. At 65 and 64 they finally had begun to do the things and see the places they had only dreamed of in their long years as part of America's faithful middle class labor force. They had accumulated no great wealth. But they had saved regularly over the years. He had been with the Sherwin Williams Company when he retired and "Mama" ended several decades of bookkeeping for a local business in their home town.

They have seen Europe a couple of times. Everybody over there was wonderful, he said. Everything was beautiful and exciting except in Paris. Paris was dirty. The sheets in the hotels appeared not to have been changed in weeks. It had nauseated the man who sat before me in the crisp clean clothes with one of the warmest countenances that I have encountered in a long time. He would not go back there, he said.

In fact, he doesn't want to go back to Europe or any other part of the world now. He only wants to see more of America. Virginia is his favorite state and Thomas Jefferson's home his favorite historical site.

Next year, he, "mama," and her sister, who is "a couple of years younger," are going out west again. He wants to see the Grand Canyon once more, then weave his way northward from there. Another glimpse of Lake Louise would be nice, too, and he urged me to see it if I ever get the chance. And take in Toronto, too, he said. It's beautiful and the people are so nice.

I wondered at all the "nice" people he had met all over the world. I waited for him to criticize someone somewhere. It didn't happen. Only the dirty sheets and streets in Paris had left him with no desire to go back, but still he was not critical of the people.

I wondered at his countenance – at the peace, the joy, the enthusiasm which shined in his eyes and on his face. He never stood up. I wanted him to. I wanted to see if his walk told the same story his face and voice did. I suspect that it did.

You know, nothing ages us more than a lack of enthusiasm and the inability to look forward to tomorrow. When we stop planning, stop dreaming, stop hoping and sharing and appreciating, then, and only then, do we grow old.

Until then, we are young.

At 86, Mr. America, as I shall remember him since I never asked his name, is young and ambitious. I suspect he will always be young. Proof again that anti-aging formulas do not come in jars and bottles.

Oh, Missy, Be Careful – August 1993

"Oh, Missy, be careful..."

Those were his parting words to me as I walked out the sagging screen door of his little store. "The old Jew" is what he was called in that neck of the woods. He owned and operated the inviting old country store, in Bridgeboro, about eight miles from our home in South Georgia.

At sixteen, I occasionally was given the keys to the family car on Sunday afternoons. Usually, I would go visit a friend. On that particular Sunday, my friend had not been home and I am glad, because I had a nice long visit with the delightful old gentleman. He seemed a bit lonely at first and it was a well known fact that he kept pretty much to himself, a result, perhaps, of the prejudice we foolishly tolerate in a world where we should know better. I was quite drawn to him.

I'd not had my driver's permit very long and this new found independence which accompanied the little card in my purse was exhilarating. I bought an Orange Crush from the man with whom I had chosen to spend my hour of freedom and we talked at length. Or, perhaps, I talked and he listened.

To this day, I only recall one thing that he said. His parting words to me were, "Oh, Missy, be careful."

Sure, I had heard the words "be careful" many times over my years. Still, I hear those words and I say them to others often enough. But there has never been a time when they impacted my life more than that day when the old Jew said them.

Why? Oh, nothing happened to me that afternoon. I encountered no danger. There were no near accidents. I just drove back home and went to church that evening with my family as usual. Nothing out of the ordinary occurred at all.

I'm not sure why the old Jew's parting words have stayed with me. Words which seemed like an afterthought from the heart of a stranger have influenced me many times when there was no one else near to care, or to offer a word of caution. I do not know how to explain how that dear old man's words have carried more weight with me over the years than all the combined "be carefuls" of my parents, grandparents, friends and others. I don't know why it is his words that pop into my mind at just the right times, or why it is his voice I seem to hear again and again. I never even knew his name.

Why do I share this story? I tell it whenever I have the chance because I like to remind myself and others of the impact our words can have. Each and every day, every waking hour perhaps, we have the opportunity to influence the lives of others with our words or lack of them. Just words. But, oh, what power there can be, for good and evil, in just words.

It's Mother's Day Again – May 1994

Tomorrow is Mother's Day, or so the calendar tells us. Everyday has been Mother's Day for me since February 3, 1969. Then on April 11, 1971, being a mom became doubly meaningful with the birth of our second son.

This weekend brings with it a reminder of all the Mother's Day cards and gifts which my sons have made or purchased over the years. They are tucked away in drawers or on shelves where I keep special treasures they have given to their mom.

One of the more precious gifts Dean and Derrick ever gave me was presented in 1984. It was not Mother's Day or any special occasion as the calendar dictates. It was, however, one of the most extraordinary moments of my life.

It had been a normal everyday kind of day and the boys were perched on our bed for some late night conversation. The atmosphere was relaxed and talk flowed easily which is not always the case with teenagers. They were 15 and 13 years old at the time.

One comment led to another and I recall talking about some things I would do differently if I could turn back time. I spoke of wanting to be a better mother, and said I could have been if I had known 15 years earlier what I had learned up until that point about parenting.

It was just a generally good sharing time. Nothing really out of the ordinary was said or done. Nothing especially memorable happened until they said good night and headed out the door for their rooms. As he started through our doorway, Dean turned back, paused a minute, walked back over to the bed, sat down beside me and said, "Mother, I want to tell you something."

Such rare teen seriousness had my full attention. "Yes?" I asked.

"I like me," he said. "I'm glad you are just like you are, and I'm glad you have been just like you have always been, because it has helped me to be just like I am, and I like me. Don't forget that."

I haven't and I won't because Derrick called from across the hall, "Hey! that goes for me, too; that's how I feel, too."

It's been ten years since that night. Now they are 25 and 23 years old and they remain comfortable with themselves. They like who they are and what they do. They enjoy life. I cannot ask for more.

Our sons are far from perfect. Through their school and college years there have been those who would vouch for that. I'm sure their peers in the military and the work place are also aware of their imperfections. Daniel and I have been more aware at some times than at others.

But perfection was not, and is not, a requirement for success as a parent or child, or in life in general. I feel good in knowing my two sons like themselves. They are comfortable with who they are and I am ever so thankful for that fact. What my husband and I have done "right" has been by the grace of God. It is His grace which enables us to rise above, and learn from, mistakes we make. It is that same grace which will enable our sons to do the same.

Yes, I still feel that I have made mistakes as a mother, wife, daughter... In all areas of my life, perhaps there are things I would do differently "if I had only known then what I know now." Then again, I'm not sure, because through it all I have finally learned to like me, too. Learning that has given better balance to my life and enhanced all my relationships with family and friends.

Perhaps that is the best gift my sons have ever given me. Their love for me, and the warm and respectful ways in which they demonstrate it, have helped me learn to like and to love myself better. On this Mother's Day I must make a point of thanking them for that.

Where the Wild Violets Grow – March 1995
A couple of weeks ago, my husband and I had an occasion to drive through Newton, Georgia, and Baker County. We repeatedly strayed off the beaten path in order to gain a better understanding of what the Flood of the Century did to that little community. It was a devastating, lonely sight we saw.

We had heard so much about the water line on the court house and homes in the area. We had seen pictures. Yet, nothing had prepared us for the emptiness we encountered. Shells of homes with tires and cans and other garbage dotted the landscape, debris left behind by the swirling waters. A town swept away.

Then, last weekend, the two of us went down to some property in Butts County on the Ocmulgee River – land that my husband leases for hunting. We took the four-wheeler, a couple of cans of sardines, saltines and iced tea and made a delightful memory of a warm pre-Spring afternoon.

We parked the truck close to the entrance to the property and walked around the area where we camped with our sons when they were small. "Jackson" is what the site was called although it is several miles south of the town by that same name. It was a second weekend home for my family for more than a decade. Then the paper company bought it and no more camping was allowed.

We climbed on the wheeler and meandered through woods that teased us with signs of budding foliage. Parking on a high bank that overlooked the river, we made our way down to the water's edge. There, we gained a closer look at the changes which had occurred with last year's record breaking rains.

There were signs of deer and turkey all over the place, and a raccoon track or two. All the while, I was anxious to go in search of the violets – the most enormous wild violets I've ever seen that grow a few acres south of where we were standing. I was curious to know what the flooding waters had done to their domain.

Again, like when we drove through Newton, I was unprepared for what I would witness. Where the waters of the mighty Flint had left drab desolation in that little South Georgia town, the Ocmulgee had only enhanced this place of serene beauty where the wild violets grow.

We stood hypnotically at the top of the little hill, hesitant to walk among the magnificent swirled markings in the sandy bottom below. The torrential rains that swept the state last year and left two mighty rivers swollen with rage had left only beauty behind in the sand where the violets grow.

We had to search for them as it is still a little early in the season for a mass debut. My husband found the first one, picked it and ceremoniously handed me an impressive bouquet. It was tinier than I have ever seen, yet still painted with the same rich velvety purple I remember from years past.

I carried it around for a while between my thumb and forefinger, then tucked it into the inside pocket of my denim jacket, near the heart that was beating with joyful thanksgiving for the lovely afternoon my husband and I were sharing.

Today, as I recall the two afternoons, and the two contrasting settings, I am amazed at the comparison between Newton and "Jackson."

Where nature had wreaked only desolation in one area forcing evacuation of its inhabitants, it had left a more majestic than ever upon which the magnificent violets are now appearing.

Surely, anybody who ever doubted what forty days and forty nights of rain could do to the earth has had those doubts erased over the past few years. Downpours have taken their toll across our land, not just in Georgia, but in Los Angeles, and all along the Mississippi. Still, the water falls in California and many residents of that normally fair and sunny state continue to suffer.

Yet, if we look for them, we find silver linings behind the clouds of life. The flawlessly beautiful acreage where the wild violets grow attest to that truth.

On Picking Up Strangers – June 1995

A reader called this week to say she identified with last Saturday's column. "Especially during the summer," she said, "company just has a way of showing up all the time."

We talked a while about what it will be like next summer – with the Olympics and all. Shucks, some of us might as well look into renting campers and buying tents to set up in our yards. Cousins and uncles and aunts and friends from way back when – we know they are all gonna show!

I told my caller how my mother always taught me that I could be entertaining "angels unaware," so I should never turn anybody away from my heart and home. For the most part, my dad never had too much to say on the subject although he, too, never met a stranger. Then came that day in 1967 when he had a lot to say.

A few days before Daddy spoke to me, I stopped for a man (actually, he was a really good-looking young airman!) who was hitchhiking on the Sylvester highway and I gave him a ride into Albany, GA.

To show his appreciation, he went to my father who worked at Turner Air Force Base where he was stationed. He told my dad what I had done and how helpful I had been, but *also* how he had worried about me and hoped I did not make a habit of picking up strangers.

Can you believe he did that? My dad had a serious talk with me and discouraged what he thought was only a budding habit. Little did he know it was already deeply ingrained.

And you know what? He and my mom entertained strangers until their dying days. So, what can I say? Actions speak louder than words, right?

Certainly, times have changed since my mom encouraged me to welcome anybody and everybody into my heart and home. Yet, caution, like anything else, can be carried to extreme. We would all do well to remember that many a stranger along the way is only a friend we haven't met *yet*.

The Surprise – November 1995
He deserved it.

For twenty-seven years of marriage and 37 years of his life he has spent his birthday in the woods. On several occasions he has been on out-of-state hunting trips. There were a few times when I packed lunch and a birthday cake and drove to the hunting land he has leased in Butts County for the past 25 years.

I have never complained. After all, it's his birthday, he should spend it the way he likes. But this year, he turned fifty and I decided it should be special. So I told him I had invited our two sons, daughter-in-law and grandson as well as his sister and brother-in-law (the brother-in-law was his mentor and has been his favorite hunting partner since he was thirteen). I led my husband to believe that his sister and I would bring a picnic lunch and meet the others at our farm in Meriwether County.

And that we did. BUT, we were joined by other members of his family and mine from all over the state. From Bainbridge, Albany, Baconton, Dawson, Savannah, Fort Valley, Cleveland, Fayetteville, and Atlanta, as well as from New Jersey and Pennsylvania, carloads of well-wishers came to surprise the one who thought he couldn't be surprised.

We met Sheriff Dan Branch and Deputy Steve Whitlock in Gay, Georgia. They led the convoy out to our property. We drove very slowly, emergency lights flashing, so as not to develop a gap in the train. Much to our amazement, oncoming traffic stopped and, in some cases, pulled off to the side of the road out of respect for what I am sure looked a little like a funeral procession at first glance.

In fact, as Daniel sat unsuspectingly around the campfire he commented to his brother-in-law about the approaching funeral procession – until we all started to turn into the pasture, that is, and he saw that my car was directly behind the deputy's, followed by friends and family and several of his fellow employees. As we slipped dozens and dozens of balloons out our windows, we knew we were well on our way towards experiencing a day to be remembered.

Glorious weather prevailed. Exactly what I had hoped for, mid 60's with enough of a breeze to make us appreciate a small campfire. Tasty fried chicken, ham and barbecue. Sandwiches, salads and beans. Cakes and cookies and pies and the perfect "hunter's birthday cake" prepared by Sue Bailey of Fairburn. Yet, the week before had held its moments.

On Tuesday, before the party, we had gravel poured on the newly constructed drive into the property. The young driver, who was dispatched to pour it, had only dumped gravel on construction sites and did not know how to adjust his chains and truck so as to spread it somewhat evenly along the drive.

Therefore, on Tuesday afternoon, with my unsuspecting husband working until dark every day, we had an impassable drive piled high with gravel, and lots of cars scheduled to pass over it within a few short days. So I called Larry Bailey, owner of the Concrete Supply Company, and told him what had happened.

On Thursday morning, he personally took a tractor down to straighten out everything. He did a fine job at no additional cost. But there's more! On Wednesday of this week he called to ask how the party went and if I was pleased with the drive. I assured him that we were indeed pleased and that the day had turned out to be everything I had hoped it would be.

Then came the near disaster of Friday evening. Only hours before the balloon blowing and cooking and packing would start at daybreak, I was at the Georgia Baptist Urgent Care Center in Fayetteville with Daniel's buddy who had flown down from Philadelphia for the party. He and I had gotten food poisoning earlier in the day at a local fast food restaurant. But Dr. Terry Rice, and all the staff at the center, made it all bearable. After treatment and a couple of hours under their watchful eye, we returned home to continue our secret preparation for the big day.

It is so wonderful to know there are still folks like those at the Concrete Supply Company who go the extra mile to please, to solve problems and make every effort possible to satisfy customers. And, professionals like those at Georgia Baptist Urgent Care who go above and beyond the call of duty, delivering service with a smile and other amenities, certainly do their part as well to make life easier and happier for all of us!

So my columnist's hat goes off this week to Sheriff Dan Branch and staff, Dr. Terry Rice and staff, Sue Bailey and her phenomenal culinary talent, Larry Bailey, as well as all the many friends and relatives who helped me pull off the most unforgettable birthday my husband has every had. In fact, he says it was the happiest day of his life.

It Was Her Dumplings I Wanted – May 1996
I made chicken and dumplings again this week. Chicken and dumplings and almost anything chocolate are my comfort foods. Chocolate reigned solitary until my mother died a few years ago.

I miss her more and more. We never achieved the kind of closeness and friendship I know we both always wanted. On the day that she lay dying, the charge nurse called the hospital chaplain to come and visit with my sister and me. She talked with us for a couple of hours and prayed for us and Mary. That's what she called my mom in her prayer that day.

We were gathered at Mother's bedside and she prayed for all the kids, and for Mary. I thought it sounded strange to hear her called that. She was Mother, and she was dying. Then and now, our grief focused on what could have been. When I miss her, I want chicken and dumplings.

Slowly, the months since her death have allowed me to call up good memories of years past, to claim the beauty and joy that comes with those happier, more peaceful times. As they surface, I find I am able to let go of more and more pain. It's called healing, I suppose. It takes time; it is hard, but it is good.

I don't think my dumplings turned out so well this week. I had made a double batch a few weeks ago and froze half of the little rolled and cut squares. Mother did that, and her frozen creations were always as good as the ones she made fresh. Not so with mine. Mine tasted more like tough noodles than fat, tender and juicy dumplings. And I over-cooked my chicken, too.

I had a lot on my mind. I was at the computer most of the day at one end of my home, the opposite end from where the kitchen is located. Time gets away from me when I am in my office. The chicken cooked a long time. Too long.

Today, as I write this, it occurs to me that nothing I could have done, or not done, to my most recent effort to make chicken and dumplings, could have made the final results perfect this week. I think I just miss her a little too much right now. It was her dumplings I wanted; there is no substitute.

I suppose I ought to tell you why I was in such need of a big dose of comfort food. A good friend who has ALS (Lou Gehrig's disease) called me the day before to tell me his case manager had told him it would soon be the end.

"The end?" I asked. "The end of what? The study program? The end of the experimental drug therapy?"

"No, the end of my life," he said.

I started to sob. I fell apart inside and out. After we hung up, I cried uncontrollably for a long, long time. I went to the bathroom, got in the shower and stayed there until I ran out of hot water and tears.

He is the one who cannot walk, is having trouble breathing, and has refused the equipment that could breathe for him for a while. Yet, he had attempted to comfort me.

ALS is cruel. It robs you of your strength. Then it takes away your ability to function in every way we come to know as normal. Finally, as it gains speed in its attack on the body's neuromuscular system, it takes one's ability to breathe. The diaphragm won't move anymore. The muscles that enable one to talk and breathe just stop working. All this while the brain is not only unaffected, but actually sharper than ever in some cases.

That night, I phoned my friend to apologize for falling apart earlier. He assured me that no apology was necessary. I told him I was angry, downright mad, and that I felt helpless. He told me not to worry, that God was in control.

In control, I wondered silently, and I suppose he heard me. He continued, "I reckon I have always felt like God was in control, in the good times and the bad. Even when I thought I was in control, I suppose I know now that He was, and He still is."

It was the next morning, when I went to the grocery to buy the chicken. I cooked the critter all day long. I wanted to beat the walls and scream, but I cooked chicken. My friend said my chicken and dumplings were "pretty darn good."

Holding No Candle to the Likes of Her – June 1996
It's been a while since I told you about one of our wild weekends. Since I am still recovering, and the memory of it is so fresh in my mind, I shall attempt to share with you a few details.

It was a calm, quiet Friday morning. I had just finished my column for last weekend when the phone rang. My brother, Darrell, in another state, was excited; a friend had just given him a couple of tickets to the Braves Game (that night), "We're heading your way. Can we sleep over?"

"Of course," I said.

A few minutes later, my sister (one of the many) called from South Georgia, "On Sunday, I'm meeting Michelle (her daughter) at your house so we can swap cars." Michelle's car had been in the shop and my sister had experienced nightmares for two weeks about the condition her Riviera would be in when it came back from the EKU campus.

"Come on," I said. "I'd love to have you."

A few minutes later, she called again.

"Is it all right if I come on up in the morning (Saturday morning) and bring Aunt Maybelle with me?"

"All right? Of course it's all right. I cannot tell you how honored I would be."

Though I had longed for her to come over the years, Aunt Maybelle had never been to my home before. And so the weekend began.

As I tend to spread various projects all over my home, at the bar in the kitchen, in and around my favorite chair in the living room and on the ottoman, in my spare bedroom, etc., there was work to be done. I had to disassemble all work stations that were not in my office, where they belong, and where I gave out of room years ago, and attempt to get my house in some kind of order for Aunt Maybelle.

I suppose all families have an Aunt Maybelle and there may be those aunts who can compare to mine, but I am sure none can surpass her. A minute stick of dynamite and a joy beyond description is what she is.

Next week, Aunt Maybelle will be 78 years young. At a shade over five feet tall and 114 pounds she's fatter than I've ever seen her, but the extra weight does not slow her down. Widowed in the early 1980's, she could write volumes on taking things in stride.

With energy beyond compare and a sense of humor like you can't imagine, excitement just radiates from her whole being. I've lost count of the quilts she's made in recent years. And nobody would attempt to keep a record of the cakes she's baked. Known far and wide for her kitchen talent, hers is a down home style that can't be beat! She has a reputation all over town (Blakely, GA), from the post office to the utilities department to the nursing homes, where she is forever delivering cakes or cookies. But no where does she shine brighter than in her gardens, vegetables and flowers! I suppose Southern Living just hasn't found her yet; that's the only reason I can fathom why she hasn't been featured.

Did I forget to tell you, she just retired last year from her actual "job." Sixty-five meant nothing to her. Apparently, 78 doesn't impress her much either. We took her down to our farm in Meriwether County to pick blackberries on Saturday in the almost unbearable heat. In childlike glee over the berries she gathered to make a pie, she literally walked circles around my husband and me. She's been Proverbs 31 in action for as long as I can remember!

Now, back to my brother from out of state... When they left town so abruptly to make it to the ball game on time, they told no one where they were going. They did leave a message on their answering machine for their son: "We've gone to Atlanta to a Braves game, will be back tomorrow." However, only the "We've gone to..." part was actually accepted by the recording device.

So, son comes in and finds the apparently unfinished message, followed by five messages from officials at a credit card company trying to contact my brother about what they suspect to be a stolen credit card. Son calls friends and neighbors. Nobody knows his parents' whereabouts. Son calls cops who listen to recording, search house and find my brother's wife's handbag with her Driver's License, etc. in it. The police put out an APB for the couple and the church family starts a prayer chain.

All this, while all us "younguns" are trying to keep up with Aunt Maybelle. We didn't succeed; never could we pull off such a monumental task. Actually, I doubt that anybody in my generation will ever hold a candle to the likes of her.

Where She Learned Simplicity – July 1996

It's about 12 inches wide and 24 inches high, brown yarn woven through a plastic backing. At the bottom, at the base of three white crosses stitched in white yarn, are a couple of yellow and green flowers. Up in the right corner floats the white outline of an angel holding forth a trumpet which appears to blast the words, also in white yarn: *Only one life, it will soon be past. Only what's done for Christ will last.*

In my youth, those words consumed me. Still, they haunt me, soothe me, excite me, numb me.

The wall hanging was a gift from my mother a decade or so ago. When she gave it to me she said she didn't think I'd hang it. "I know it looks like something a child would do," she said. And it does.

Many of the things my mother did looked like something a child would do her Easter bunny cakes, her Christmas trees, her wall decorations. Depending on the season and my mother's whims, those decorations might consist of little stick crosses made of cake icing or twigs from the yard or crayon marks. The crayon creations were made by little hands other than my mother's – little hands whose hearts had first heard about Jesus while sitting on my mother's lap.

Her entire life was dotted with childlike remembrances of the cross of Jesus Christ. All who entered her home were reminded of that hill some 2000 years ago on which her Savior died. Of course, she always let you know about His empty tomb, too!

Jesus, I suppose, was the theme of her life. Jesus and a childlikeness that followed her all her days. "Except ye become as little children," Jesus had said... "ye shall not see the kingdom of God."

And so, as a child she did come and go from the throne of her Heavenly Father – forever and always prayerfully taking her loved ones before Him in simple faith, acknowledging the fact that He loved them even more than she did!

Sometimes, kids tend to look to their parents for things they don't get. I thought I needed more stability, strength and consistency. Jesus was what I got. As it turns out, Jesus was enough.

Who was I to think I knew what I needed? I had decades ahead of me to add a little order and discipline to this thing called life that God gave me. Life He had given me through the mother who made sure I knew it was from Him that I had come and to Him I would one day return. She never really gave herself or my dad much credit for having all those babies. We all came direct from God, she said with knowing conviction. It's just the way it was. Who was I to question such calm and simple wisdom?

Simple wisdom it was. At her death, all her earthly belongings would have almost fit into a large car or station wagon, but, still, she left a legacy. She left reminders of Jesus in the margins of her Bibles, (she wore out several). On the pages of stained, crumpled letters she mailed to us over the years Jesus was always mentioned. In the collections of news and magazine clippings she had marked up over time were notes about "what God can do." These priceless mementoes filled boxes which somehow survived the many moves she made over the years.

And she left a few wall hangings like the one over my desk to remind those who see it or hear about it, that we have only one life here on this earth, that it will soon be past, and truly, only what is done for Christ will last.

And what is it that we can do for Jesus Christ?

Again, the answer is simple. He summed it up beautifully when He told His followers that the greatest commandment was to love the Lord God with all our hearts, souls and minds; and then He said the second commandment was to love our neighbor as ourselves. Those tablets of stone had never been so well condensed. He did have a way of simplifying things. Could be that my mom learned simplicity from a master teacher.

Rejoicing Over Second Chances – August 1996
I had the absolutely awesome opportunity to attempt to explore a mountain this week with my sister, Tamra. An attempt is all it was because within the first hour, I knew it would take a lifetime to uncover a sampling of the secrets of Hogan's Mountain. Nevertheless, I made a gallant effort in the short time allotted.

By late morning of our second day, at the wheel of an accommodating little red and blue four-wheeler, slowly and expectantly, I began to make my way to the top. There, delicate wildflowers adorned with a variety of butterflies welcomed me to their humble home. Massive black and grey stones draped against a canvas of dew smitten green grass provided the ultimate furnishings for the creatures who abide there. The clouds which seemed so far away from down below were now a close ceiling to this heavenly abode. To the east, the grand old Carolina town of Asheville nodded a distant greeting.

Have you ever been to the top of a mountain? If so, did you stand there as I did and gaze solemnly down again at where you came from? On the mountain peak, only the present moment exists. Yesterday's cares and heartaches fall by the way as you make your way to the summit. And the glorious thing about climbing a real mountain is that you can go back down again and stop off at all the places you didn't have time for on the way up.

That's not always true about life though, is it? A "successful" rise to fame does not often afford such luxury. On the road paved with lofty, sometimes mistaken aspirations we may be lonely, but we are seldom alone. Others climb, too, toward what they perceive to be success. We use blinders to aid us in setting our sights on high-minded goals. Blinders and lofty goals are not always good for us.

Isn't it wonderful the way life gives us so many second chances?

The couple who invited us to the mountain knows about second chances. A year ago, a viral infection attacked his heart and killed the pace at which they were living. But the man lives on and the woman he loves rejoices. Atop their beloved mountain their spirits soar and the love of their youth is rekindled yet again.

Too often, the closed doors of life paralyze us with regret and bitterness. Only when those closed doors leave us no further choices, however, are such responses understandable. And that's never, because, always, we have choices. If we don't get caught in the web of regret over the past, our choices can make of the present and even the future something even more beautiful than what the past afforded us.

Because Your Load Looked Heavy – October 1996
Carol Davis was in Nashville, Tennessee for a business conference. She was exhausted as is often the case after flying in early in the morning, spending the day getting an exhibit set up, and otherwise preparing for the work that always lies ahead at such conferences.

She was staying at the Gaylord Opryland Hotel and took a cab to another part of the city for dinner. Upon returning to the hotel she retired to her room to rest from a long and weary day. Within minutes she realized she had left her change purse containing more than $100 in the cab.

Having lived in New York City for ten years, it never occurred to her to call the cab company and ask if it had been found, reported, turned in, etc.

Not hardly!

However, the next morning she was talking to someone at the hotel about what had happened. Her listener was a Nashville native who urged her to contact the cab company. After arguing for a time about the futility of the call, she finally agreed to make it.

The change purse had been turned in. The company had been waiting for her to contact them and would send a cab driver to return it to her that day.

Carol was speechless.

Speechless, that is, until later in the day after the purse had actually been returned with all her money inside. Then she started telling her story to everybody. She couldn't stop talking about the experience. And to top it all off, the cab driver would not even accept a reward! He could not do that, he had said, because he was just "doing the right thing."

Sometimes the act alone is its own reward...

If you are ever in Nashville and need a taxi consider calling American Rivergate Taxi Service.

And...

Working at the Opryland Hotel, there was this tall, beautiful woman with skin that shined like black silk and an unforgettably bright smile that shined even brighter. She left *me* somewhat speechless.

If you ever have had the opportunity to stay among this grand expanse of rooms you know how quickly you can begin to feel like you are in a maze as you try to find your way around. The gardens and the river that runs through one atrium after another are simply spectacular. The sheer size alone of the complex threatens to be overwhelming, yet somehow your stay remains totally enjoyable *unless you are attempting to walk what seems like an endless mile from your room to your car while carrying a very heavy box of books.*

My sister, niece and I were making our way through the seemingly never ending facility when we realized we had lost our way. We did not have the opportunity to ask for assistance. The staff doesn't give you much of a chance to do that there. It appears that they are trained to watch for expressions such as ours and offer to help at the first sign of need.

This beautiful lady with the long black braids asked if she could help us. We asked her to tell us how to find the Cascades canopy entrance around from the main entrance. She reached to take the heavy box of books from my niece and said, "Follow me."

"I can carry this. Just show us the way," my niece protested. The box was really heavy and we had already realized that we should have called a bellman. Pride being what it is, we were well on our way and thus determined to make it on our own, but independence would not rule the hour.

The box of books changed hands in a flash. Protests were ignored. We followed as this young woman, with the friendly smile and strong back, hoisted the box onto the side of her hips and set off at a light and happy pace. We wound through corridors, up an elevator that seemed to appear from nowhere and around a couple of corners until she stopped and handed back the box. "Just continue down this hall and you will come to the exit," she said.

My niece had a roll of green ready to thrust into the hand of this Samaritan. "Heavens no, I can't accept that," she said. "I just helped you out 'cause your load looked too heavy."

It had been four years since I was last in Nashville; I don't think it will be so long before I return.

Aunt Audrey – November 1996

Aunt Audrey died this week. I haven't slept well since I received the news. She was in her eighties and hers was a good life. Always a hard worker, she lived on the farm in South Georgia when her children were small. Then the family moved to the Florida.

There, she and Uncle Carlton continued to tend a productive garden almost year round. You know... "you can take the girl out of the country, but you can't take the country out of the girl." That garden, and the love behind it, made her meals unbeatable; her door was always open to family and friends – always, any time of the day or night and for any length of stay. She was a rare breed.

In Florida, she worked in a fruit processing plant for many years. Every effort was made to be sure her hours away from home coincided with those her children were away, as well. After all, her family, immediate and extended, was what life was all about.

Her only daughter, Delores, had been killed in a tragic automobile accident while Aunt Audrey was in her early sixties. A mother, father and four brothers grieved. An endless stream of family and friends wept with them. It was Aunt Audrey's faith that carried her through that loss. Actually, her faith sustained her through more than a few losses and tremendous struggles.

I remember well her smile, her lightheartedness, her warmth, her consistent evenness... Okay, so maybe I just invented a new word to describe Aunt Audrey; she deserves it. By evenness, I mean she appeared to never be at the mercy of uncontrollable circumstances. I recall no highs and lows or gripping ups and downs of spirit or personality. Maybe it was just her faith anchored in the roots of hard work and good clean living that made her shine. Oh, and another thing, she was discreet. Discretion, a rare attribute, goes a long way with me.

I received the call from her son, Bruce, on Tuesday morning. That evening, around 8:30 p.m., I was traveling on Georgia Highway 85, just south of Fayetteville. Alone in my car, with a heavy heart and a knot in my throat, suddenly a young doe darted in front of me. I braked, but it was too late. The thud, which still rings in my ears, ended the life of the graceful night traveler.

With that sound, an era of my life seemed to end as well. Like an exclamation point used to close a sentence that would have preferred a simple period, the shocking thump of the deer's body against my car reminded me just how quickly the end of many things can come.

I cried for the loss of my mother, father, grandparents, uncles, aunts, cousins, friends and the young deer. So great was my sense of loss that no sleep came throughout the night.

Through glazed eyes I watched the election returns. Well into the early morning hours, I lay in bed listening to mini speeches of victory and concession delivered on the voices of hoarse, spent politicians. And I recalled years gone by.

I heard again the ring of Aunt Audrey's voice welcoming me into her home. My dad's robust laughter knocked on the doors of the empty, aching chambers of my heart. Mother's prayers echoed powerfully in the corners of my consciousness. The eternal twinkle in my grandfather's blue eyes traveled across great chasms to comfort me as only he could.

Yesteryear's hugs, words, gentle smiles, laughter, tears and prayers sprinkled themselves upon me as magic star dust on a clear spring night. Though sleep never came, I reveled in the warmth and security of love that never dies.

For many, Tuesday marked the election of an array of politicians who will lead us – proudly and, perhaps, not so proudly – into the next century. I suppose it was a sleepless night for great numbers of people, a night for both losers and winners to try to let go and move on. Surely, it was a night that asked us to celebrate the promise of tomorrow.

For me, Tuesday marked the near end of an era in which the road I now travel was hewn. I feel a monumental gratitude for those who took the time to plant the flowers, shrubs and grand old trees whose eternal and encouraging form, bloom and fragrance ever mark my path. Though an era may be coming to an end, still tomorrow calls. I will respond by moving forward with a renewed sense of thanksgiving in my heart for those whose lives and love helped to make me what I am today, and will be tomorrow.

Though the beloved seed planters must leave us behind for a season, we who remain in this realm will continue to reap the harvest of their labors. I hope they know how much we appreciate their efforts.

Tomorrow Calls

Tomorrow calls
and our destination beckons,
yet to meander down memory lane
and pause for a moment or two
at the doorway of yesterday
is a luxury we can ill afford to turn down.
Alas! To walk through that door again
is forbidden now.
Though it was the chosen road back then
we shall travel it no more
except in memory.
Oh! There will always be those September days
when we will recall the many paths
which once lay before us,
and the choices we made,
and the voices we heard calling us –
voices which still may softly call today.
Ah, yes! Tomorrow!
Where an untraveled path awaits those
who would keep on traveling,
dauntless and unafraid,
knowing the price they paid will be worth it all
when tomorrow comes.
When all the regrets of yesterday
have seemed to fade
into the grandest sunset of all the ages
tomorrow will come
and the sun will shine on a new day
a day in which we will, at last,
see as we are even now seen
and know as we have always been known
a day when we will have reached our destination
and
finally found our way home.

Ending the Conspiracy – March 1997

I was quite young, no more than five or six years old, but I remember well the first time I reached for Papa's hand and caught hold of the hot cigarette. It was also the day he bought me my first Coca Cola. We were about to walk up the stairs at the hospital to see my mother who was ill at the time and had been hospitalized a few days earlier.

My hand burned and I cried. The Coke was supposed to calm me down. I think it must have worked because, today, the feel of that ice cold beverage in my hand and the way it burned and tingled in a nice, refreshing way is a more vivid memory than the burned hand.

Other cigarette memories, however, remain painfully intense. I suppose they will never go away. A few years before she died, I told my mother of one memory. She said I must have been no more than three years old and was surprised at how accurately I recalled the time.

It was early morning and we had just finished breakfast. In the bright and glorious way it announces the beginning of a new day, a soft stream of sunlight was filtering into the room through the kitchen window. Daddy lit a cigarette. I started to cough. I begged him to put it out.

He didn't.

He was already addicted.

Daddy started smoking when he was stationed in India during World War II. He drank a lot while he was overseas as well. When he returned home, he never touched another bottle of liquor, but he didn't put down the cigarettes until after his first open heart surgery.

He was addicted.

I recall how furious his surgeon was after the surgery. Apparently, Daddy had told him that he had not smoked for months, that he had left the cigarettes alone after he experienced the first heart attack. He had lied. The truth surfaced with the horrendous post-op struggle my dad experienced.

He had been addicted.

His older brother, also a smoker, had died a decade or so earlier. A stroke had taken him out rather abruptly. It didn't happen like that for Daddy. He lived ten years after his first open heart surgery, but the damage was done, and he never fully regained his health. The blockages continued and open heart surgery did not work the second time around. I don't think there was ever a moment that he did not want a cigarette.

Because he was addicted.

After he responded to what he perceived as a call to preach the gospel, and attended seminary in the early sixties, he wanted to give up his cigarettes. And, oh, how he tried! The only thing he succeeded at was hiding them in his pants pocket and hiding himself when he just had to have one.

Since he was addicted.

My dad's brother and sister, the non-smokers, now are in their late seventies and continue to work full time! I love them dearly and I am so glad they are still alive.

Yet I am bitter. I try not to be, but I am.

You see, the first two decades of my life were miserable, at times, due to severe asthma. At age twenty-three, I had lung surgery, after which the surgeon came to my hospital room and said, "If you don't quit smoking you could be dead in five years." Then he left the room.

I cried uncontrollably for hours. Finally, the charge nurse called the doctor back to the hospital to straighten out the mess he had made of my emotions, and my breathing, after I finally told her I had never smoked a cigarette in my life.

The doctor was most apologetic. He explained how hard that was to believe since my lungs showed such evidence of smoke inhalation. My husband stopped smoking that week. And no one has been permitted to light up in our home since.

So, folks, I reckon I can say I felt good this week when the Liggett Group, the manufacturers of the very cigarettes smoked by my dad, and his dad before him, finally conceded that their product was addictive and causes health problems.

What an understatement. Sometimes, more often than not, in fact, I am more than amazed at the lack of just plain common sense in this world. Truly, it is an uncommon commodity.

It did my heart good to hear Arizona Attorney General Grant Woods say, ``I believe this is the beginning of the end for this conspiracy of lies and deception that has been perpetrated on the American public by the tobacco companies. Somebody is finally telling the truth."

The truth...

The truth can be therapeutic, but it won't bring back my dad nor erase all the years I suffered before I finally gained the courage to forbid smoking in my home. Neither will a lawsuit. But I do feel good about the settlement reached last week between Liggett and 22 attorneys general in the suit they filed against the industry to recoup Medicaid health care costs of treating smokers. It is a beginning.

My Princess Is Dead – September 1997
We moved to Albany, GA when I was seven years old. I started third grade there, and at eight years old I had my first published writing appear in a Christmas special section of The Albany Herald. That also was when I discovered the Carnegie Library, mythology and fairy tales. I don't recall the first fairy tale I read, but I do recall well my infatuation with the pages that would transport me to other worlds, other times, other realities. Every week, the librarian would help me search for new stories of fantasy and romance, kings and queens, princes and princesses.

I never knew the day would come when one of my characters would become real. Sure, I knew there were queens, kings and princesses in the world. But not like in my fairy tales. At least, not until Diana. Not until Diana did I believe a real princess existed.

Note that "real" is the key word here. Alive, tactile, vulnerable. Touching. Hugging. Laughing. Crying. A saint one day and a sinner the next. Yes, she was real, and all the world has watched for a decade and a half as her story has been written on the pages of every newspaper and magazine known to man.

For the reality of all she was to end so tragically in an automobile crash in which alcohol played such a major role has left me feeling sick inside. I am one who is so susceptible to the influence of drugs and alcohol that I require pediatric doses of medications which sedate or stimulate.

Oh, I have heard all the arguments. Everyone is different, I am told. Some boast a tolerance so great that no amount of liquor renders them incapable of driving. Baloney, I say! Still others have told me that they actually drive more carefully after a few drinks – that they are the safest drivers on the road after a couple of beers. Give me a break!

My, how we do like to defend our vices. But my princess is dead, and I fear I will have less tolerance than ever now for drinking and driving. I am sick of hearing about the photographers who are being investigated as a cause of the accident that killed my princess. Sure they were always hanging around her. Though they were certainly a mixed blessing, they were not a curse. Their photographs fed the world's ever increasing infatuation with her. And it was our undying love and admiration that gave her the power she had come to know and was learning to use more wisely and well.

The hungry, the poor, and the dying around the world had sensed her concern for them. She had reached out and touched the untouchable many times. She had made us believe we could do it, too.

Assuredly, the media around the world needs more systems of checks and balances. We need to maintain some degree of respect for the right to privacy that every individual deserves to one degree or another. There is no doubt that privacy becomes a rare commodity once a person comes under the scrutiny of the press, either by fate, birth or choice. But more than one fortune has been made by such media attention. More than one cause has been rallied behind by throngs of people because of the media. And more than one drunk driver has been taken from behind the wheel of a car, before he could kill again, because the media made his sin known to a reading public who demanded action.

Our princess is dead, as is her friend, and the drunk driver who was behind the wheel of the car in which they all perished. It is too late for them. It is not too late for you and me, my loved ones and yours. Don't drink and drive.

The Price

There is a price
one pays for fame...
a cost, be it small or great,
to have a recognizable name.
To aspire to heights unknown,
to never stop
until the summit of each mountain
is claimed, and to look down again
is not all it's cracked up to be;
for along the way, a while ago
back at some near-forgotten bend
there was a little house
by the side of the road
where stayed one
who lived in the shadows
and longed to be my friend;
but I lingered not,
for I had a ways to go
ere the day should end
and now I cannot go back.
Oh! The fields lie painted
with rainbow colors before me
and breathtakingly beautiful
is the expanse of the heavens
I now can see.
Fulfilled I should be
my promise unbreached
but somewhere
just down the hill and back a ways
my heart stayed
and
it was a high price I paid.

Being There for the Birthing and the Dying – November 1997

From the birthing to the dying and for every special occasion in between, she's there for her family and friends.

On the job too, she takes responsibility farther than most of us. As an associate manager in the American General (AIG) office in Bainbridge, she works with a number of agents as well as a far greater number of clients who know Lynda will be there for them (Lynda, the Christmas tree sister, as you have come to know her over the years, with a tree in every room of her house from Halloween to New Year's.)

Unique is what she is. A blessing to us all. And that's what last Saturday turned out to be as well. A real blessing.

Never idle, and always one step ahead of all who know her, Lynda put together the ultimate family day. In March of this year, she purchased a few dozen tickets to Swamp Gravy and set about getting the family together to attend.

The acclaimed Swamp Gravy theatrical play is performed six or eight times in the spring and then repeated again in the fall, in the little southwest Georgia town of Colquitt where I was born. I will tell you more about Swamp Gravy at a later date; for now, I want to tell you more about Lynda and what she means to me and my family.

As the day of our gathering for Swamp Gravy drew near, Lynda informed my siblings and nieces and nephews, and even an exchange student from Brazil, who is living with my brother and his family for a year, that Aunt Maybelle would be cooking dinner for us on Saturday.

We would eat at 3 pm, visit for a while, go by the cemetery in Colquitt at 6:30 to pay respects to our mom and dad, then proceed to Cotton Hall just off the square for the 7:30 performance.

Afterwards we would walk over to Tarrer, a beautiful old hotel on the southwest corner of the square. It is recently restored and magnificent! Again, I will tell you more later.

This is the way Lynda does things. Every detail is taken care of personally. I don't know how she pulls it off day in and day out!

Sometimes I am convinced she must have been cloned a decade or so ago. She even attends the funerals of her clients when they die and encourages her agents do the same!

It is part of her ministry, I suppose. Oh, she just calls it her job; but nobody takes responsibility to the degree that Lynda does, so I call it a ministry.

When asked, she even sings and plays the piano at funerals. I'm sure she holds some kind of record for funeral attendance and participation.

Yes, the birthing and the dying and everything in between finds her there. In between is what last Saturday was.

When we all gathered at Aunt Maybelle's home in Blakely we were in awe once more at the astonishing energy of this aunt who will be 80 next July. As agile as a child (really!) she keeps a yard full of flowers that would cause any avid gardener to be envious.

Well known far and wide for her cooking and baking, she bakes hundreds of cakes throughout the years for families and friends who request them. She cans vegetables and fruits whenever they are in season, and in her spare time, she quilts. Her first craft show is coming up soon. The woman is amazing. As is my sister, Lynda.

And they were both in all their glory as family gathered on Saturday to enjoy food and fellowship. It was food to the tune of creamed corn, green beans, candied yams, pickled peaches, potato salad, turnip greens, pear salad, fried chicken, sugared carrots, homemade biscuits (no other kind bakes under her roof) and the best, absolutely THE best, chocolate cake you ever tasted.

The exchange student from Brazil who only likes America's macaroni and cheese, rice and shrimp was flabbergasted as Aunt Maybelle insisted she "just taste" everything. It was assuredly an unforgettable day.

One of the most heartwarming moments occurred as Lynda and I stood in the living room at Aunt Maybelle's, watching as Jimmy and Beth walked towards the house for lunch. Jimmy is Aunt Maybelle's youngest child. Now is his mid fifties, we watched him stride towards the house with that same excitement and energy his mama is famous for.

"Look," Lynda said, "look how she still looks at him." And I looked to see a bride and groom of 35 years who clearly were still in love. We looked long enough to be sure he still looked at her the same way. We were not disappointed. And then the laughter began. Jimmy would have it no other way.

Do you know how awesome it is for large families to get together for fun not just the birthing and the dying, but just plain fun? Lynda does. That's why she makes it happen.

I Only Thought I Was Tough – January 1998
I thought I was so tough. I thought I could move back to the country, go back in time and relish every waking and sleeping moment. Ah... not so!

From December 13 until January 7, we had no television reception. None.

So enamored was I of the awesome opportunity to commune with God and his creation in the midst of the great outdoors that I didn't miss the constant jabbering and endless commercials, at all. At first...

I was well on the way to finding my own measure of Thoreau's bliss until that eighth or tenth day when I plugged in the set and nothing happened. I mean nothing.

I just wanted to watch the news. See a weather map. Maybe catch one quick spin of the Wheel. Just one peek.

It was not to be.

Okay, I can deal with this, I said. At least for a while, then we'll call and order one of those 150 to 200 dollar satellite dishes and join the rest of the world again.

So I dealt with my retreat from civilization for a while longer. The VCR works well so we watched every old movie we own, even bought a couple of new ones.

But the claustrophobia continued to build. That's right, claustrophobia. That's the only way I know how to describe it. I was feeling more and more shut off from the world. Even the Internet didn't ease the smothery feeling.

So I called to order the $200 satellite.

Not hardly!

Since my greatest *need* was for local news I was told it would cost between $750 and $979 to hook us up for such reception by satellite.

No way was I going to pay that kind of money for a piece of metal or plastic or whatever those little dishes are made of when we have a tractor to pay for, and seeds to buy for a spring garden, and a multitude of wildflowers to purchase for the front pasture... (My brother laughs when I talk about planting wild flowers, assuring me that if *I* plant the seeds they will not be *wild*flowers...)

I could not convince myself to spend almost a thousand dollars on television reception. So I went to WalMart and bought a little set of RCA "rabbit ears." I cannot tell you how excited I was on the drive home. Anticipation was building. I drove a shade faster than the speed limit in order to reach home for the 6:00 news. I could hear the TV calling my name, commanding me to relax in my favorite chair and watch and listen...

Within seconds of my arrival, Daniel and I plugged up our little set of rabbit ears, then excitedly pushed the power button.

Then the channel buttons.

One after another...

Nothing happened until we hit channel 11! Then there she was! Brenda Wood! My favorite anchor! Could it be? Could we only pick up one channel with our new rabbit ears, and was it to be the channel on which I could watch Brenda Wood? And The Wheel? Another miracle!

Of course, I shall watch them on a snowy screen, not unlike the one of my youth when I lived with my family of nine in the middle of nowhere. And that is a major factor that caused this piece of land to hold such an attraction.

Both Daniel and I grew up in the country and we hail from large families that chose to live close to God and the land. We have longed for some time to provide a place for our extended families and friends to come together to celebrate the past and present with back porch singings, bonfires and wiener roasts, and ice cream makings – to enjoy nature and claim a bit of calm and quiet in this ever so busy world to which we all have evolved.

Just last night, we talked with a friend in New Jersey who is driving down over the weekend to spend some time with us in this quiet country place. He spoke of how excited he is and how much he looks forward to once more enjoying the serene setting. Just before the phone call ended he assured us he would arrive on Sunday in time to watch the games.

Perhaps our new environment will call for a bit of adjustment on the part of many a relative and friend.

Empty Promises – February 1998
My husband promises me we will have all of the boxes unpacked by the end of the year. Of course, I'm smart enough to know, with the demands his job is making on his time, that he really means I will finally have everything unpacked by the end of the year. I may be well on my way, but with spring planting season just around the corner, some boxes may go on hold for a while.

At last, however, my office is starting to feel like me again. Sterile, bare walls do nothing for my sense of creativity. Nothing at all! And I cannot write in an atmosphere of even the vaguest formality. I suppose I must like clutter. It comforts me in a strange sort of way. Organized clutter, that is. So, top priority for me has been to get my working environment productively arranged.

Finally, most of my favorite posters, clippings, and quotes that I have jotted down on whatever happened to be on hand at the time over the years, are back on my office wall. Of course, we had to finish off a portion of the attic in order for me to pull this off. Daniel would have declared war if I had begun taping and tacking my favorite things to any other wall in the house.

He turned pale when he walked in a couple of weeks ago and I announced that I had hung the window shades. Rushing to see how many brackets were straight, he had the good sense to hold his tongue. All in all, I had done a pretty good job for a first effort.

Talk about emancipation. There is something about using a complicated, noise-making gadget confiscated from your husband's off limits tool box that leaves a woman feeling like she can do anything! Almost.

I still have not been able to find a great number of things that I previously thought I could not live without. Yet, here it is two months after the day of their disappearance among all the cardboard and tape, and I'm doing just fine!

Couldn't even find my electric mixer until last week. And you know what? I have made brownies and an apple cake without the use of any power driven machine and my son says it's the best apple cake I ever baked. (And I'm known for my apple cakes! See recipe that follows.)

Could it be that simplicity will become the order of my 21st century? Ah, I hope so. You would be surprised at the things you can do without. I am, and it's nice.

But there is one thing I want more of, and this week, the tenth anniversary of my dad's death marks the beginning of that "more." We have approximately 28 to 30 friends and relatives coming for the weekend. Some have been instructed to bring sleeping bags and I probably will have to make use of the floor in my office in order to accommodate everyone, but I am beside myself!

There could be no better time than Valentine's weekend to return to a tradition I have missed terribly. I grew up with six siblings and boocoodles of cousins. There were well over a hundred "close" relatives on both my mom's and dad's sides of the family when I was just a child. Counting second and third cousins I had surpassed the 200 mark by the time I hit my early twenties.

So, the first two decades of my life were highlighted with frequent "get-togethers" the like of which I have not experienced since childhood. Now, as I near my fifth decade, that is going to change. A return to the old order is on the agenda and the excitement is indescribable! Oh, yeah! The back porch singings and ice cream makings of my youth are about to make a comeback.

My husband's mom will turn 83 on the 25th of this month. The following weekend we have 45 people coming to celebrate the occasion. Luckily, two of the families will be driving in on self contained travel trailers. With a family circle the size of ours there should be no limit to the occasions we can concoct in order to come together and just enjoy one another.

Okay, you are beginning to think I am contradicting myself when I talk of returning to a more simple life on the one hand and hosting large gatherings like this on the other. I suppose it all depends on one's state of mind. Assuredly, you must let go of some things in order to embrace others, like the need to have all the boxes unpacked and everything in order before I invite guests.

Many years ago, a friend, Anne Pille, was en route to Florida from Arizona and she showed up unexpectedly at our home in Fayetteville. The kids were small and the house was a mess and I was terribly embarrassed. But she quickly alleviated my apparent discomfort by asking me if I really thought she had driven five hundred miles out of her way just to check out my house-keeping habits. I have never forgotten her question – so let the company come.

The Apple Cake Recipe

1 ¼ cups corn oil
2 cups sugar
3 cups White Lily unbleached self-rising flour
3 large eggs
2 teaspoons vanilla
2 cups chopped apples
1 cup chopped nuts

Mix oil and sugar until sugar dissolves. Beat eggs and add to mixture. Mix well. Add flour and stir well. It will become hard to stir, but stir long and well. Add vanilla, apples and chopped nuts (I prefer walnuts or pecans). Keep stirring and mix well. When you can stir no more, pour into greased and floured tube pan (I also line the bottom of my pans with waxed paper like my mother always did.) Bake at 350 degrees for one hour and 15 minutes to an hour and 30 minutes, depending on what type of apple is used. I find that the Granny Smiths take a little longer than other varieties. Ovens also may vary.

NOTE: You can play with this recipe. Sometimes, I add a cup of coconut or use coconut flavoring, instead of vanilla. At Christmas, I have used rum flavoring. Almost any apple will do. I've had great results with Winesaps, Yorks, McIntosh and Granny Smiths, even the Red Delicious which is my favorite eating-any-time-of-the-day-or-night apple. Some folks like big hunks of apple in their cake, but I like to chop mine really small. And one more thing, sometimes I mix a couple of tablespoons of fresh orange juice into a cup of powdered confectioners sugar and glaze this cake while it is hot. Without the glaze it also is excellent served warm with whipped cream or ice cream! Have fun and enjoy!

On Profanity and Morality – March 1998

The first time I ever heard God's name used in vain I cringed. The first time I ever read the gruesome details of rape or murder I cringed. The first time I ever saw the dead body of a suicide victim I cringed. The first time I ever saw a sex scene on television I – well, maybe I did not cringe – but I sure was shocked.

Now, I don't even flinch. Seldom do any of the above scenarios stir me to "react." So commonplace is profanity, violence and mayhem that I suspect most of us have become conditioned to it.

Consider with me the implications of such conditioning.

As a young girl, I was nurtured and protected. My mother never worked outside the home and I went to church and Sunday School regularly. I had graduated from high school before I saw my first movie on the big screen. Our television viewing and reading materials were monitored, as well. Parental censorship? You bet. Did I rebel? Of course, to a degree. Basically, I was a fairly normal teenager, and teens tend to rebel.

Now, consider with me today's teens and the atmosphere in which they have grown up. Moms are working outside the home. Parents pick up their little ones from daycare in the late afternoons, and plop them in front of the set while dinner is prepared. In many instances, dinner is eaten in shifts and kids get little time for quality interaction with those who claim to love them most in the world. Quality time *is* scheduled though, since only the truly foolish parent would fail to do that.

But can you schedule quality time? Maybe *adults* can. Maybe couples can plan for and claim a few hours out of the week for real communication. Maybe they can and maybe they can't. Could be that the present divorce rate in this country is trying to tell us something. Of course, we all may be living so hard and fast that we will never get the message.

Messages *are* being passed though. The media, the real and ever present parent of the children of this country, has told us that profanity is okay, adultery commonplace and murder sensational.

All this we will discuss, as it presents itself for discussion, during the quality time we plan to spend with our children.

So many tangents beckon, it is hard to stay with the comparison I am trying to make concerning my own formative years and those of children today. I could not deny the little streak of rebellion that welled up in me as a teenager. It seemed like I had to respond and declare my own individuality. I had to distance myself to some degree from the parents who had taught me right from wrong, and attempted, to the best of their ability, to instill godly principles of living.

The distancing, or rebellion, felt natural; it did not seem wrong. At some point, we all must learn to fly on our own; and, for many, the first attempt is made during the teen years.

So, if it is natural and that distancing must come about, what happens when no values have been instilled prior to that time? What about if the only values the child has learned have come across the airwaves from movie and television studios?

I suppose we only have to pick up any newspaper in America or tune into any television network to answer that "what if?" question. As gruesome as the present day scenes are, which seem to be unfolding with a horrifying degree of regularity, I suspect they are only going to get worse.

I cringe to think – yes, I can still cringe at some things – and I do, indeed, cringe to think of what will happen to today's talk show generation. If the pathetic display of human behavior which is paraded daily across the stages of talk show hosts who are trying to outshock one another in order to gain ratings ever becomes commonplace, then America is a goner.

Of course, I have always maintained that a chain is only as strong as its weakest link, and therefore America is only as strong as its weakest family. If my summation is on, or near, target then America already may be well on the way to becoming a powerless "goner."

I do not mean for this to be another column blasting the media or Hollywood for turning the children of America into ruthless murderers. I don't think there is any need for me to attempt such consciousness raising. I suspect any sensible person would readily concede that television and movie screens across America have indeed made violence and murder so common place, and illustrated it in such minute detail, that anybody of any age can pull off most any crime these days.

I suppose I am just thankful, very thankful, that my mom stayed home with my siblings and me. Sometimes, one just has to stop and realize, "there but for the grace of God, go I..." Maybe that's all I am doing just now as I cringe at the thought of checking out today's headlines.

Scratching Peg's Bellybutton at 4:30 A.M. – March 1998
A close friend developed a sudden and severe GI (intestinal) bleed earlier this week. Her son called and said "Mama can't stand up, and the ambulance is here, and she wants you."

Within seconds, I was out the door wearing dirty jeans and a comfortable old flannel shirt that I had bought off a clearance rack in the men's department at Wal-Mart a few years ago. I had just come in from a walk, a long walk, in the woods, so, luckily, I was wearing my very favorite, worn, and cracking-all-the-way around, high top sneakers.

For nearly thirty-six hours that was my attire. In fact, I was well into my thirtieth hour, I suppose, when I realized what I must look like. A peak in the mirror confirmed my fears just about the same time I realized I had no toothbrush or make-up with me, either. Ah, but my comfortable old sneakers had seen me through.

Every woman should have an emergency kit in the trunk of her car and any female who has ever been where I was last week, and on numerous other occasions, knows what must be in that kit. Yeah, you would think I would have that kit in place by now.

It's strange how there are some things you just don't think about when a friend's in trouble. She's out of the woods now after having received a few units of blood, and we have a diagnosis. She will be all right, and that's all that matters.

I suppose she will have to change her eating habits for a while, but, at least, she's gonna be around to fuss about it. How nice it will be to hear her complain about all the pinto beans and fried cabbage and pork roast she can't eat now. Some of us would gripe because we had to eat such fare. Not Peg. Her country roots include her culinary inclinations, right along with her willingness to be there for every friend and acquaintance who calls on her. It is the way of a neighbor and friend, she says.

She's right, but she, like many of us, must realize there are far more neighbors and friends than there were a hundred years ago, or even twenty years ago. What does the ultimate caretaker do when she comes face to face with the fact that she can't do it all anymore? What does she do when she must succumb to being cared for?

She takes it less than gracefully, of course.

As I reached under the machine in the Piedmont Hospital Nuclear Medicine Department at 4:30 in the morning to scratch Peg's belly button for her, I realized anew how much control we can be forced to relinquish when illness strikes. To add insult to injury (or profound illness), the nurse on duty made some reference to Peg's daughter (me) which only reinforced how very drastically the tables can be turned.

There is only one year between us and I suppose we do look a little bit alike. Yet, on almost any given day, the average person's perception would assuredly be the other way around. Folks might not think Peg was my daughter (at least, I hope not!), but they would most certainly be more prone to think she was my younger sister.

Normally Peg has every hair in place, make-up done to perfection, a smile for everyone, and the most truly uplifting, encouraging manner in all the south. But Peg was sick. Hemorrhaging. Fatigued. Scared. Wiped out at the moment. Exhausted following the recent deaths of three members of their extended family, as well as a friend. All had died in the past thirty days. Caring for what needed caring for under such circumstances and still running her florist shop full time, while also looking after two sick members of her immediate family, had taken its toll.

Toll or no toll, we do it though, don't we? We answer the call when we are needed. All of my sisters and brothers respond to those in need in their neighborhoods and churches and beyond. It is the way of friends and family in the south. I hope it is like that everywhere. I am told it is not, but I can hope, can't I?

The Accomplice – April 1998
I had no idea how easy it could be to become an accomplice to attempted murder.

I was on my way to the back field on the fourwheeler to watch the early phases of the approaching sunset, and also to try to catch a glimpse of the turkeys (which I see all the time, almost daily, while my husband and his hunter friends find them ever so elusive).

Animals know whom to trust. At least, they did until this week, until I threw them a curve.

I still can't believe I did it. Can't figure out if I was showing off, or wanting in on the kill. Assuredly, my motives were not pure.

You see, Daniel and the guys have been upset with me for riding the fourwheeler all over the property. They think the noise scares the turkeys away.

"Not so," I have claimed repeatedly. I mean I can drive it within fifty yards of them, turn off the machine and, if I don't move, they seem to think I'm gone with the noise of the engine. (So far, I'm not terribly impressed with the intelligence of this proud, overgrown bird.)

In the opinion of this novice, the turkeys are far more leery of the tromping of human footsteps than of the purring of engines.

So, there I was about to round the curve into the back meadow when I spotted them through the trees. I topped the highest point in the field and killed my engines, all the time wondering how "those men" could kill such innocent creatures.

Then, suddenly, I remembered Daniel was on the tractor in the front field. I could scoot back up there, get him and show him how simple it is to observe the turkeys from the wheeler. I could prove to him how easy it is to fool them into thinking you're gone with the click of the engine key.

So, I cranked my machine and raced (safely) back to the front field motioning with one arm (not so safely) for Daniel to get down off the tractor and meet me out on the grass. He stopped the tractor and walked over. "Hop on," I said, "I'll take you to the birds."

Like lightning he popped off the top to the case on the wheeler that holds his shotgun (I didn't know. I did know that case was where he put his rifle when he went deer hunting, but I did NOT know that only that afternoon he had put his shotgun in it.) Almost instantly, he had it loaded and commanded me to "Drive."

I turned toward the back field and squeezed the gas lever. In less than a minute we had spotted the courting gobbler. Daniel jumped off the wheeler and headed into the thick woods after him. Within seconds, I heard the shot.

"Come look," he called. And my heart skipped a beat. Had I so easily become an accomplice to murder?

Does it happen that quickly? Can a person go from joy riding to armed robbery, attempted murder, or murder... in a little more than a flash?

But you say we are talking turkeys here, or are we? Maybe. Maybe not.

You have heard the stories just like I have. You have probably read them in the newspaper. On a dare, in a moment of drunkenness, while under the influence of drugs, or maybe just to "innocently" show off a bit, many a person has acted or reacted in ways that have ruined their lives.

Shoplifting, home burglaries, convenience store robberies – are all these crimes calculated? Does the guilty party plan for weeks or days before taking action?

Not always. Sometimes it happens in a flash, in no more time that it takes to drive from the back field to the front field.

Now, I am not equating turkey hunting with crime sprees. I am just telling you that I have never entertained the thought of killing a turkey. On the contrary, I have had a bit of aversion to doing so. But there I was. Caught up in the action. Enjoying it...

Only later, was I relieved that he had missed.

What Snuffy Taught Me – September 1998

I never understood before. Just never quite grasped how a pet could be afforded family member status equal to or greater than that of a human.

I have never been able to understand how someone could become so attached to an animal that they would spend hundreds or thousands of dollars on one that was seriously injured.

And absolutely never, not ever, did I picture myself checking for new chewies, balls, ropes, etc. on the pet center aisles at WalMart, K-Mart, Kroger and Ingles every time I shopped.

Of course, all that was before Snuffy.

As you may recall, I mentioned the little mutt one other time in this column. I told you how I enjoyed my morning walks with Snuffy the puppy, hot on my heels, and the morning dew lapping at my feet. In the early weeks and months of his time with me, we would startle the deer or turkeys when we would go walking. Later, as he grew and assumed the role of protector of the place, the only time I ever saw the wildlife up close was if he was asleep, or if I locked him in the garage. Keeping other animals at bay became top priority with him, all nine pounds of the brave little fellow.

I must tell you about his bravery. When he would hear the deer or turkeys walking in the woods just off the back yard he would bark. Not just one bark mind you. We are talking barking until he became hoarse. Barking incessantly. Barking so loud and long until it took two or three pillows over my head to drown out his effort to warn his family of the trespassers. Little did he know they had been here long before he or I had ever set foot on the property.

Occasionally, we would go out on the porch and try to soothe Snuffy. We would encourage him to be quiet and try to persuade him that all was well. Mostly, we would just stand in the bay windows and peek at his little trembling body as he paced the porch in his protective ritual that could not be squashed. Only if we opened the door did he dart into the yard with a remarkable ferociousness totally inappropriate for his tiny frame, looking back over his shoulder to be sure we were witnessing the risk he was taking for us!

There was no risk, real or imagined, involved on our walk last Saturday morning, however. It was early, with little traffic out at the road to disturb the serenity of the hour. The grass was still wet with dew as we made our way through the yard and down the trail in the woods to the creek. When we came back up the trail, he pouted for a time while I sat in the swing under the old oak tree. Then he ran and got his knotted and ragged little rope in an effort to coax me up to play keep away or fetch. He always would define the game, or games, moment by moment.

How was I to know the moments would be so few?

That afternoon, two Labrador retrievers from across the road were turned out for their daily run. That day, they ran across the road to our place. It was the first time six-month-old Snuffy had met a neighbor animal and he was beside himself! So much so that he ignored Daniel's call to him as he set out to follow the animals back home. It was nearly a thousand feet to the road and Snuffy had never ventured there before. The danger was unknown.

The thick privet hedge across the front of our property prevented him from seeing the accident, but the squealing tires caused Daniel's heart to skip a beat. He and Dean jumped in the truck to go check out the scene. The Labs had made it safely across the road. Snuffy did not.

His nose was scratched and he had trouble standing. Daniel gingerly picked him up and brought him to the house. I paged the vet who agreed to meet us at the clinic. Snuffy's spine was broken in three places. His back legs were paralyzed. On Monday, we agreed to have him put to sleep at the Vet's strong recommendation.

I didn't know I still had any tears left at that point. The decision to let him go brought more tears. They keep coming. I miss his obnoxious little bark, his wet paws on my clean jeans, his tiny brown wire-haired face peeping through the bay window to observe my every move. I will never again make fun of another pet owner who is overly attached to his or her dog, cat, horse or any other animal. I am sorry I ever did. I miss Snuffy.

When Frankie Died – November 1998
They called him Frankie. He was the jailer at a small county prison in rural South Georgia. In his early fifties, he had quietly and faithfully served in that capacity for years. He was well liked by the inmates who were stunned when Frankie collapsed and died at the prison time clock last week. The prisoners took up a collection among themselves to buy flowers for Frankie's funeral.

It was a small grave side service. Only a few friends and close family were present. There were brief words and a prayer. While a friend of the family sang "I Want To Stroll Over Heaven With You," the wind rustled the leaves of the trees and the canopy flapped in harmony. Then the wind grew still as the voice stopped singing. Some in attendance say it was a strange, even eerie, experience.

But it was the word from the prisoners who made the small group doubly aware of how very special was the man whose body they were laying to rest. Along with the flowers from Frankie's former charges was a note: "He fed us when we were hungry. He gave us something to drink when we were thirsty."

By all accounts, Frankie was not a man of means. In fact, he apparently had struggled all his life to make ends meet, and had spent the last few years living with his mother. Her heart is broken. Her loss is great. As is mine and yours.

Mine and yours?

We never met Frankie. Never even heard of him until this week. Right? How can you or I miss him or his quiet influence?

How can we not? We always will miss those who feed those who are hungry and share a drink with those who are thirsty.

All of society benefits from the compassion and generosity of such individuals. We never know when or even if the cycle will end. Perhaps it never does. When one gives of himself or herself to another, sooner or later the recipient will pass it on. It is one of the finer laws of life that affects all of us.

Jim and Me – January 1999

Twenty years ago, or somewhere thereabouts, a week or so before Christmas, my friend Judy received a two pound box of Russell Stover chocolate covered nuts from a Bell South (then Southern Bell) co-worker.

While we visited with Judy and family over the holidays, she and I hid with the delightful box two or three times. Out of sight, sound and smell of all others, we indulged ourselves. We shared with no one.

I'm not especially proud of the fact, but I'm not ashamed either of being a chocoholic from way back. Of course, more and more I am realizing that I may not be a true addict since I tend to pig out only on good chocolate.

I don't know if Russell Stover is the best or not, I just know it is REALLY good. I suppose I will never know if it is truly the product, or those wonderful stolen moments I had with my friend a couple of decades ago, that has made the candy part of my holiday tradition.

Until this year, that is. Since we finally have gone "back to the country" where our hearts have been all along, it is a 45 minute drive to the nearest place that sells Russell Stover chocolates.

Oh, I meant to get them. They were on my list, and I was in Fayetteville on Wednesday the 16th before the Holt Family Christmas at my house on Saturday the 19th. That would have been the perfect time to hide and indulge myself, with thirty-five relatives milling about throughout the house. I have a big closet. I could have pulled it off. Ah, yes.

But it was not be. Jim Minter has ruined my twenty year tradition. I haven't even craved my chocolates this year. At last, I realize it was not the candy, but the secrecy that I loved so well.

This year, I am sneaking around the house enjoying stolen moments with Jim.

I wanted to wait. I did not want to even see his book until after the holidays. I knew I would be hooked. If I ever saw it and touched it, then I would have to read. There could be no waiting until there was more time. Some things are like that, you know – like a good box of chocolates.

But there I was in the Banks Crossing Shopping Center walking from Belk's to Kroger and it called my name as I walked past Bookland. I briefly fought the urge one last time. I lost.

Thus, ten days or so before Christmas were spent sneaking around the house with Jim. On two nights, when my husband was sick with some sort of flu thing that he was afraid I would catch, I slept in the guest room upstairs with Jim. I read into the wee hours of the night. Could never eat those chocolates for that long. When the alarm went off, you guessed it, I rolled over and grabbed Jim. I was compelled.

By dawn, I had decided every high school in the south should make Jim part of their required reading program!

This guy can build a fire on the pages of a book, not with the pages, mind you, but with words on the pages that make you want to hold your hands out for warming. You can almost taste the marshmallows he roasts over the coals. And the way he defines the finest of Cuban cigars (the H. Upton which he says was no longer obtainable after Castro took over) inspires this allergic asthmatic to almost long for one exotic whiff.

But the most wonderful thing about the written word that flows from Jim Minter's hand is it makes me laugh. I mean it makes me laugh inside and out, alone or in a crowd. Not everyone, in fact, very few writers or entertainers or just plain people, can make me laugh a lot. And I like to laugh.

Jim Minter, distinguished newspaper man extraordinaire, yet country boy from the top of his head to the soles of his feet, has given every true southerner, and deserving transplant, a gift for all seasons with the writing and publishing of "Some Things I Wish We Wouldn't Forget (and others I wish we could)."

Another thing about this wonderful book, it has not caused me to gain an ounce! I wonder if Jim could deliver another one by next Christmas. My bathroom scales would be most appreciative.

Dylan and Me – January 1999
I picked up my grandson, Dylan, on Tuesday afternoon with a promise to have him back home in 24 hours or so. We spotted seven deer on the ride home. Guthrie met us with mixed emotions; I never knew dogs could be so jealous. We ate only what we wanted to for supper: chicken and ginger snap cookies. Then we built a Lego house, and watched no TV. It was nice.

At bed time, the stories began. I told one. He told one. My turn again. Then his. Until I fell asleep. I am sure he soon followed. The story ritual (he much prefers the ones I make up over a book) is always the way we drift off to dreamland where he goes to meet Mommy. For a four-year-old ("just turned four" he reminds all who ask his age), 24 hours is a long time to be away from mom.

Morning came and our adventures began again. First, a quick, informal business meeting and one other necessary appointment. Then, in the car, I asked Dylan if he would like a special treat for lunch. Of course his answer was yes, but neither of us had any way of knowing how very special our next couple of hours would be.

I had recently heard about The Isabella, in Jackson, Georgia, from friends who said I must go there, that they were certain I would love it. No real details. "Just go the first chance you get" were my instructions.

The chance had come. We headed for Jackson.

On State Highway 16, I drove a couple of blocks east of the square and glanced off to my left to spot the grand old Victorian home. Ah, my friends were right, we were about to go back in time.

The entrance was breathtaking. We were soon seated at one of the best tables in the house. Dylan, in his mismatched sweats, never once complained about not being properly dressed. In fact, in a matter of seconds, he gallantly rose to the occasion when he reached for an oversized goblet of water, gingerly lifted it and said, "Bonjour, madam."

That was a first. Then with the goblet precariously balanced in his little hands, he said, "Oops we forgot to bump our glasses."

"Bump our glasses?"

"Yes, Gangan, we need to touch our glasses when I say 'Bonjour.'"

Indeed, life is an adventure.

The food was spectacularly prepared and presented! The service warm and friendly. We were made to feel more than welcome, even a bit spoiled. With him being the only kid in the place, I was fully aware that the experience could have gone in any number of directions. Elaine Dunn, the owner, told us we could walk about a bit after lunch and explore the upstairs if we liked.

We liked! Until we ran into the chef who asked if we had seen the ghost. Dylan's only response, "Me is ready to go. Now! Gangan, let's go now."

The upstairs adventure was over.

Back downstairs, Elaine asked how we liked the tour. It was great, I said, until the chef mentioned the ghost.

"Me no like ghosts," the little one promptly piped.

We soon left, but not without having gleaned a bit of history about the place. George and Elaine Dunn purchased the lovely home in 1985 and lived there until a year or so ago when they decided to turn it into a restaurant and share it again with others.

I say "again" because it had been in the McCallum family for a hundred years prior to the Dunn's purchase and was opened to the community on many occasions over time. Flower shows were held there and even a high school prom or two.

Upon returning home from the Civil War, John McCallum set about making a small fortune for himself and his family. His prosperity allowed him to purchase 200 acres upon which he constructed the two story, ten thousand square foot home. Ever so grand in its day, it remains a treat for all who enter.

And the ghost? Luckily, on the day we visited, she was in the basement or perhaps out in the garden or... Oh, well, don't let her existence keep you from checking out The Isabella. The house alone deserves the trip, but the food makes it doubly worth the drive. I had fried crab cakes over pasta with fresh Parmesan and a medley of vegetables on the side. I understand they have a seafood buffet on Friday nights which I hope to try soon.

On the brochure I picked up on my way out, I read these words, "It is our pleasure to share the beauty of a bygone era with you and your family and friends. It is our prayer that you will enjoy your meal and will share the beauty of this home with others."

Some things just are not meant to be kept to one's self. I am glad George and Elaine Dunn recognized that fact, and I trust that their prayer will be answered many times over.

What My Heart Considers – March 1999
It is March 26th. It is my mother's birthday. It is also the anniversary of her death. Strange how we tie things in to all those anniversaries of our lives, isn't it? As I go through all the motions my day requires in order to achieve the goals and deadlines the calendar requires, I must pause to consider what my heart requires.

Maybe the heartache would diminish a bit if I called a halt to all the day's scheduled activities and made chicken and dumplings. Such comfort! Then the house would at least smell like she was still around. Or maybe I could try to make one of her chocolate cakes. I've never tried in the past. Why make the effort if I know in advance it could never taste like hers did?

Better yet, with Easter just around the corner, I could go out and purchase every colorful bunny and chicken I could find at a nearby Dollar Store and set them up all around my house and yard. Of course the dining room table would have to be covered with them as well. In the center of the table would be a grand cake made in the shape of an empty cross and every plastic creature would be turned to look toward that cross. And wherever there was a bunny or chicken in any other part of the house or yard there would be something there to symbolize an empty cross as well.

My mother knew what Easter was all about and any yellow, green, pink or blue anything that made its way on the premises had to compete with that empty cross. The cross may have been made of twigs, framed needlework, embroidered pillows or whatever she fancied any given year, but it always was the center of the Easter celebration. It all began weeks before Easter Sunday. The colorful plastic stuff was for the children – the children who would some day ask about that empty cross.

But the adults could not get away from the message she sought to convey either. Her strategy was perfect. She clipped every poem she ever read about the death and resurrection of Jesus Christ, and if you went to the toilet in her house you had to see them. Of course, she could not force anyone to read, but, if you ever sat down on a john on the premises, they were there right in your line of vision. So well posted. And that wasn't just at Easter; her postings went on year round.

My mother never had a problem mixing a celebration of the Resurrection with an Easter Egg Hunt. It was all part of celebrating new life. All the bright colors and spring blooms and new clothes –you would be amazed how she tied it all together.

No holiday ever meant more to my mother than Easter. Even Christmas couldn't hold a candle to Easter Sunday. "Without Easter, Christmas would mean nothing," she always said.

As a young child I never could quite grasp that "born to die" concept which connected Christmas to Easter. To further complicate things, my mother would always point out, "Not just born to die, but born to die and live again, forever," she'd say.

I've told you before how I used to have trouble with Jesus. I just could not quite grasp the fact that He was God's only begotten son, born to live and die for all creation, then arise from the grave to ascend into the heavens and live for all eternity. And he did it all, my mother said, for me. I think that may have been the part that I had the most trouble with.

For me. It was easier to think He lived and died and lived again for the whole world than to imagine that He did it all for me. But I learned over time that it didn't matter one iota if I believed He did it for all the world, if I did not believe He did it for me.

Yes, I miss my mother. But I have Jesus, and because of Him and all He did for me, I know I will see my mother again one day.

I can't really erase my calendar. I have work to do and I will do it. And I really don't want to go buy a lot of plastic stuff to set around my house either. But that toilet, that's another thing. I have lots of poems and devotional books and... I believe I feel a decorating urge coming on. Anything could happen in the next few days. Between this anniversary of my mother's birth and death and the celebration Easter affords us, my bathrooms could take on a whole new look!

Is There a Doctor Aboard? – May 1999
She was a transplant from Boston who had fallen in love with a South Georgia boy stationed in her city back in the 1960's. When he returned home she came with him. Her first job was with Southern Bell as a split shift operator. In February of this year, she retired from her position as an engineer with the company.

I met her thirty years ago at a dove shoot at the farm owned by her husband's family. She became an instant friend of the forever variety. She and I took our first vacation together last week. Just the two of us. We went to Los Angeles.

Judy had never been to the west coast, so that's why we decided LA was where we ought to go on our special vacation. We scheduled our trip to coincide with several book shows going on out there. She collects antique cook books. Inspirational books are my favorite. We were not to be disappointed on our book treks, shopping trips, or sightseeing ventures. Our star-gazing left a lot to be desired, however. Can you believe she even insisted I drive down the alley between a row of stars' homes in hopes of catching a decent glimpse of "somebody"?

I will never admit to driving down that alley. But I will tell you we saw some of the most beautiful flowers you could ever imagine. Every born and bred Georgia girl knows Thomasville is the Rose Capital, but though our lovely old South Georgia town can certainly hold its own, I fear it can't beat LA in May. We saw roses as big a dinner plate. All the usual reds and pinks, plus lavender and peach and snow white. Yes, snow white, there was no smog while we were in town. It was strange. The natives said the wind and rain that preceded our visit had cleaned the air. We could see for miles.

One day, we drove up the coast to Malibu and wondered what kept all those massive houses – stacked haphazardly, like multicolored match boxes – anchored to the sides of the hills. We learned that a "big" lot near the ocean (65 feet wide) could be ours for just under a million dollars. It was not prime property so we passed up the offer!

The multimillion dollar digs of Beverly Hills were perched on lots not much wider than those near the ocean. Streets far too narrow for this claustrophobic Georgia girl enticed us into the Coldwater Canyon area. Would you believe we drove by homes where you could almost ring the doorbell from your car?

By day three, I was already wanting to get back to the wide open spaces of home. There was no way I could imagine, at that point, just how very happy I would be to set foot on Georgia soil again. As it turned out, I was back in my beloved state for several hours before my feet could actually touch the ground.

You see, we were met at the Atlanta Airport by an ambulance that transported me to Piedmont hospital. I had become quite ill during the flight. At one point, I was asked if I wanted the pilot to put down in Oklahoma (only hours before a string of tornadoes would touch down unexpectedly). Once the flight attendants had managed to lay me down across three seats in the middle of the big jet there had been considerable improvement in the excruciating abdominal pain. I no longer thought I was dying and opted to ride it out.

Melinda, one of the flight attendants, knelt by my side and prayed me home. My friend held my hand all the way. Tori, the nurse who had responded when there was no doctor on board, was almost angelic. Audrey, the Delta "red coat" who met the plane, along with my faithful and frantic friend, Barbara, was awesome.

If Audrey is any example of the folks who wear those red coats at Delta Air Lines, the company has even more going for it than I have thought over the years. My opinion has never been bad. Today, it's never been better.

I do not recall hearing the name of the pilot who got us to Atlanta ahead of schedule. I wasn't the only sick soul on board. There was a man in the very back who had symptoms similar to mine. Luckily, we both had refused the Oklahoma City stop.

With sincere thanks and a prayer that God will return to all of them a double measure of what they gave to me on Monday, May 3, 1999, my columnist's hat goes off to the Delta flight crew, the emergency response team who met us at the gate, the staff at Piedmont Hospital's emergency room and my personal physicians. Surgery is scheduled for later this month to correct the problem that caused my unforgettable ride on Flight 266. In the meantime, I have a few more walks to take on the old Georgia dirt that means more to me now than ever.

Oh, and one more thing, those "coincidences beyond imagination" that dot my path, assuring me there is a God and that He cares about every detail of our lives – they fell like raindrops on May 3, 1999.

Saving Sybil – March 2000
I don't know if she's still alive as I write this. Never even heard her name until last night. It's Sybil. Had no idea who she was, where

she was from, what her life has been like. But, yesterday, in a very small way, I shared what she was going through.

Life. It's strange, isn't it? The chords that tie total strangers together can fall from nowhere to wind knots never to be broken again.

It all started with a dream I had night before last. I was in a motel room with a sick friend and Lynda, my sister, unexpectedly opened the door and walked in.

I awoke and could not put the dream out of my mind.

By mid morning, I put on the T. Graham Brown CD that I had recently purchased. I had been saying I was going to buy the CD for 12 years. Finally, a sense of urgency had gripped me earlier this week. I searched through Best Buy and Media Play until I found it.

Twelve years ago, while standing by my dying father's bedside for a week at Tallahassee Memorial Hospital, my sister and I heard that T. Graham Brown was having a concert in town. We fantasized about leaving the hospital for just a few hours to go hear him. Of course we never left Daddy's side, but there was something about the fantasy that gave us relief. Go figure.

Anyway, I buy the CD this week. Finally. And yesterday I played it over and over and over while thoughts of the Tallahassee hospital and Lynda kept dancing in and out of my mind.

By 4 p.m., my anxiety level was almost through the roof. I knew I wasn't dealing with some strange kind of flashback. I had begun to fear for Lynda's welfare.

I called her office first. They just said she wasn't in. Between 4 p.m. and 10 p.m. I called her cell phone about 12 times, another sister, a brother, and Lynda's husband. Nobody I talked to knew where she was. They did not even seem concerned. All I could do was pray.

Shortly after 10 p.m. I became calm enough that I could lie down on my bed and rest. Sleep was out of the question, but I thought I could rest.

At 11:30 p.m. my phone rang. Lynda was calling from her car. That morning, she had insisted that a hotel clerk in Bainbridge let her into the room of a friend and business associate from out of town who had not shown up at the office on time. She had immediately taken the friend to a local hospital. Doctors at that hospital had called for emergency transport to Tallahassee Memorial Hospital where her life hangs in the balance at this writing because of a leaking aneurysm.

Why do I tell you this story? Because I can never remind you often enough how short earth life can be. Because we must always be open to the many ways that we (stranger and friend alike) are drawn to one another. And we must, absolutely must, be willing to bloom where we are planted. And you and I do not always control (if ever) where we may be planted and when we must bloom.

My sister has a very demanding job and she had a thousand things on her plate yesterday. None of it mattered. Nothing mattered except getting help for someone in need. She could not even think of herself, her work, or her own family, until the woman's husband had arrived at the Florida hospital last night. Then, and only then, could she walk away from the situation.

And only then (around 10 p.m.) was I able to become calm, lie down, and relax until she called. I knew she would phone as soon as she got word I had been trying to reach her.

"Did you listen to your messages? Who told you I've been calling?" I asked.

"Nobody. I just knew I had to call you the minute I got to my phone. It's been locked in my car all day at the hotel, or I would have called you earlier so you could have been praying."

Like I had not been all day.

Ah, yes, the ties that bind. A Henry County woman on a business trip to Bainbridge. My sister who tosses reason to the wind when her little voice (I think it's the same voice I listen to. Angels? The Holy Spirit? ESP?) tells her something is wrong with that woman. And I, totally uninformed, feeling all the turmoil and anxiety of the day, wanting to escape as I did 12 years ago, but praying instead, while listening to T. Graham Brown in the background.

Don't even try to figure it out. I gave up years ago. Just go with the flow. Bloom where you are planted. And pray.

Elise and Me – March 2000

She will not be two years old until June, and she is not old enough to leave home, but she thinks she is. Twice she has spent the night with me. Eternal nights.

The first one was a few months back and she had to do it because big brother was going to do it. This time, last night, was the result of a week or so of "Granengan's house, pease?"

On the last visit (the all-nighter, that is) somewhere around 3 a.m. I decided there would be no more of doing it because big brother did, she would have to beg before she spent the night with me again.

After her recent days of "Granengan's house, pease?" which surely came across as begging, she came again.

Oh, my...

I suppose we slept some. I just don't know when. She was tired and actually asked for "bed, now" early, so we retired shortly after 9 p.m. We just didn't stay down for very long.

"Dark now."
"Light back on."
"Juice, pease."
"Dark 'gin now."
"Light back on."
"More juice, pease."
"Dark 'gin now."
"Light back on."
"Ant bites hurt, kiss 'em."

Finally, we dozed again. Until Bunny had to have some loving. And of course I had to wake up and give it to him. There's a fuzzy little duck stuck to Bunny's ear (Bunny was once an Easter basket rabbit) and I can't tell you how many times the duck on Bunny's ear got kissed last night. We took turns forever, until I began to beg, "Dark now, please?"

She eventually agreed. She even dozed at one point. Then the words arose once more from the bundle of warmth tucked under my arm, "Light on now, juice pease."

More juice it was.

More juice means more diaper changes, of course. There were four during the night. At this writing, as she sits here on my lap pointing to the keys I should hit, I can't recall how many more times we were up and down during the dark hours while big brother and Granddaddy slept soundly downstairs.

And the source of most of the misery I feel this morning? I was not allowed to turn away from her. I tried to do so repeatedly. "Back" she would say, sweetly entreating me to turn back over towards her before she would grab my shoulder and attempt to force the issue. At one point, she inserted a tiny forefinger inside my bottom lip like a fish hook and held on fast until she dozed off again.

At other times during the night, when I would attempt to doze, that same little hand would finger my face, whispering softly, "Nose, mouf, eye, ear." The ear was definitely her favorite spot. I'm sure she knew every little dip and curve long before daybreak.

Oddly enough, it was around daybreak before she finally dozed into what appeared to be deep sleep. For two hours, we lay there in quiet bliss, until suddenly I heard the voice again, "Downstairs, now."

She is no worse for the wear. I, on the other hand, will feel the effects of the night for days, and enjoy the memory for years.

I was talking with someone earlier this week about what it means to be wealthy. He said it means being able to pay bills on time, eat well and enjoy life.

And here I am, now, in this moment, realizing anew that it's nights like last night that give me gladness of heart and make me wealthy. Brief moments, hours, days/nights spent with family and friends, giving birth to memories that last forever, and making all of us rich beyond measure.

The Henry County, Georgia woman (Sybil) that I wrote about last week is still fighting for her life. Valiantly from what I hear.

Keep praying. They are going to try to take her off the respirator today. My sister thinks a miracle is in the making. Sybil's husband, family and friends are with her, encouraging, stroking, praying, standing by her. In America today, that alone is a miracle. We all should rejoice, as we keep praying.

Following Sybil's Progress – March 2000
When I called today to check on Sybil, Lynda said Sybil's husband reported yesterday that his wife had said "Hi" to her therapist. Such a little word and, and only one at that, but all those who love Sybil rejoiced. It will be a long row to hoe, but Sybil is alive and on her way to being well again. I understand she soon will be moved from the Tallahassee hospital to Piedmont Hospital or the Shepherd Center in Atlanta.

After responding to the little voice inside her heart that insisted she check on Sybil and get medical help for her, Lynda is looking at her often misunderstood gift/s in a whole new light.

For those of you who have not been following this column in recent weeks: Sybil was on a business trip to Bainbridge. She did not show up for an 8 a.m. meeting at Lynda's office. My sister reasoned that it was probably an allergy thing, that Sybil probably had taken something for allergy and just overslept.

Reason soon got tossed out the window, because Lynda's little voice kept telling her something was seriously wrong. Lynda drove to the hotel and insisted that the attendant let her into Sybil's room where she found her co-worker seriously ill and took her to the hospital. Sybil had developed a leaking aneurysm during the night and her life was hanging in the balance.

When I spoke with Lynda this morning, my sister said, "God has already given us so much. Lent is a time to ask ourselves what we have done with these gifts..." She was reading from a morning devotional book. She said the supporting Scripture was Matthew 21:33-43.

I checked it out. It is the parable of the landowner. It is potent. Read it. And while you do, remember the words my sister tossed my way this morning, "God has already given us so much. Lent is a time to ask ourselves what we have done with these gifts."

She is struggling still with her gift. We both have struggled with it all our lives. I like to think we have more than one spiritual gift and I hope we use them wisely. But there is this one that we have always questioned. Seems we got tossed something a little stronger than your basic intuition. When the little voice inside our hearts says "do" or "don't, "go" or "stay," "act" or "don't act," we have learned that we darn well better listen.

I blew it again, just recently. I called a friend, Cindy Foley, about ten days ago. She could not talk long as she was heading out the door for a tennis match. Instantly, I wanted to tell her not to go. Of course, I did not, it would have sounded like I wanted her to stay and talk to me instead of going to play tennis. I bit my tongue. She tore her Achilles tendon on the court and spent the next day in surgery. Now, she is confined to her bedroom for a spell.

Did I know what was going to happen to Cindy? No, I just knew I should tell her not to go. She does not know me well enough to have "listened" to any word of caution I might have tossed her way. My sons, on the other hand, who have seen my warnings play out again and again, now listen. It's about time!

The truth is it's hard to speak up when you have nothing to support what you are saying. I mean, if you are about to warn someone of what might, or will, happen if they do or do not do a thing, and if they listen to you and follow any suggestions you offer, then nobody ever knows what might have happened if they had not followed your suggestions. See what I mean?

It takes courage to speak up. I do not know what to call this gift. I only know that I am learning to listen to my little voice even when all reason, all the facts, and all well intended advice do not agree with that voice. Should I be stroked and told how courageous I am for doing so? Not hardly. Only I know how many times I have ever so cowardly backed away from using my "gift."

The truth is I act on it now more than I used to in order to avoid feeling bad later for not acting after events unfold that could have been avoided IF I had acted. Read Matthew 21:33-43 sometime soon and consider anew what gifts you have and how you are using them.

If you don't know what your spiritual gifts are, read Romans 12:6 and the twelfth chapter of I Corinthians. And as you read, be ready to be reminded how much we all need one another. Any time we fail to be all we can be, and use the gifts wisely that we have been given, others suffer, and we do, too. Does God love us any less? No, I don't think so, but in the end, we may love ourselves a bit less, if we refuse to be all we can be and use wisely the gifts we have been given.

Meeting Sybil – April 2000

I met Sybil yesterday and I may never be the same again.

Do you remember how I said earlier that prayer changes things? I know that it does. I cannot prove that it does. I cannot convince any other being of the power of prayer. Even when one hears a prayer being offered up to God and watches events unfold in direct answer to that prayer, even then there are those who will rationalize the whole scenario. I've been there. I know.

I've also prayed, that is, communed with God, and watched miracles unfold after participating in such a powerful act. And I have stood in absolute awe and indescribable wonderment while observing the forces that come into play when prayer is the catalyst. So, again, I know.

Well, meeting Sybil allowed me to live the truth of both avenues of knowing.

Recall with me one more time Sybil's story. An insurance professional for 32 years, she was in Bainbridge to train a new customer service rep, when she did not show up as scheduled on Thursday morning. To make a long story short, my sister went to the hotel to check on Sybil, was assured she was okay, that she was just sleeping in. Lynda walked to her car to leave. As she reached for the door handle, her hand would not work. It would not touch the handle. She could not open the door. I don't mean she chose not to open the door; I mean, like magnets pushing against one another, her hand and the door would not meet. A little inner voice said, "Go back."

She went back and insisted (and when Lynda insists on something, oh well...). Once she was in the hotel room, (yep, complete invasion of privacy here) she realized Sybil was quite ill. She rushed her to the nearest hospital where she was immediately transported to Tallahassee Memorial Hospital. For well over 24 hours, there was some question about whether or not Sybil would even survive.

But not with Lynda. She knew Sybil would live. I tried to prepare her for the fact that she may never be "normal" again, even if she lived. My sister would not hear of it. "You don't understand," she would say. "God would not have opened so many doors just to slam the last one in our faces."

Now, I didn't especially like her answer. I know too many people who remain paralyzed or brain damaged or even comatose following ruptured aneurysms, accidents or serious illness. So, I, the nurse, was trying to prepare Lynda for less than a perfect outcome. Lynda, the prayer warrior, however, knew better.

Looks like Lynda, the prayer warrior, won out this time. Sybil's doing great! I met with her yesterday at Piedmont Hospital in Atlanta. I saw her. I touched her. I laughed with her. I felt like Thomas demanding to see the nail-scarred hands.

Later in the day Lynda said to me, "You still don't get it do you? I barely knew Sybil before all this happened. I did not have any kind of inside scoop. God just led me to intervene and then to pray for her."

And so Lynda prayed. All that day and through the night while Sybil's life hung in the balance, she prayed. After spending the entire day breaking into a hotel room, racing to hospitals, and standing vigil with family members, she went home at midnight to sit at her breakfast table until dawn where she cried and prayed for Sybil, who was not even a close friend, just a business associate she hardly knew.

Lynda was right. I just didn't get it.

In an effort to make me understand, Lynda directed me to Romans 8:25-27: "...if we hope for what we do not see, with perseverance we wait eagerly for it. And in the same way, the Spirit also helps our weakness; for we do not know how to pray as we should, but the Spirit Himself intercedes for us with groanings too deep for words; and He who searches the hearts knows what the mind of the Spirit is, because He intercedes for the saints according to the will of God..." (NAS)

Lynda's words ring in my ear and heart: "I didn't have any inside scoop. All I know is that for a brief 24 hour period, I was listening, I obeyed, and Sybil is alive and well today. I only wonder now how many opportunities I have missed in my lifetime because I wasn't listening. I am changed forever because of that 24 hour period and the opportunity I had to experience what intercession really means."

Lynda is not the only one who's changed. I saw Sybil yesterday.

The Ultimate Frozen Stress Buster – July 2000
If you read me regularly you know I have offered a great many stress busting tips and relaxation techniques over the years. And, if you know me, you know why I'm always looking for new ones.

Am I wired? Sometimes, but not often. Mostly I just overextend. Could be that oldest kid syndrome, along with a few other quirks I've picked up over the past fifty years. But I won't bore you today with how I got to be me. What I want to share is one of the neatest stress busters I've ever discovered.

NOTE – I do not recommend this on a regular basis. In fact, whatever mental health (stress reduction) benefits you gain from the awesome experience of doing it probably will be physically neutralized by what you are actually doing. But don't let that little tidbit keep you from enjoying what I am about to suggest.

Ready?

If you don't have an ice cream freezer, you are going to have to buy or borrow one for this treat of treats. And don't forget the ice cream salt, table salt just doesn't cut it.

Ingredients for the ice cream (not the stress busting technique – that's coming later):
- four eggs (I prefer fresh ones straight from my chicken pen)
- one and one-half cups sugar
- one tablespoon self-rising unbleached flour
- instant pudding (3.9 oz - chocolate)
- one can sweetened condensed milk
- one can evaporated milk
- four mashed ripe bananas
- whole milk
- one teaspoon vanilla

Combine sugar, flour and evaporated milk in saucepan over medium heat. Mix well with electric mixer. Add pudding and mix, mix, mix. Don't walk away. Keep stirred while heating for approximately eight to ten minutes. Do not boil. Add well-beaten eggs. Stir and stir and stir for another couple of minutes. Remove from heat. Add sweetened condensed milk and mix well. Add vanilla and mix. Stir in mashed ripe bananas and continue mixing well with electric mixer. Pour into four quart ice cream freezer. Finish filling to marker with milk and stir well. Place in freezer for one to two hours to chill. Remove from freezer and get started turning the crank (the best way), or plug in your ice cream freezer if it's electric. Use ice cream salt liberally on the ice in the freezer and of course, follow the direction that come with your machine.

NOW... When it gets too hard to turn, or when it automatically cuts off if it's an electric machine, let it set for a few minutes. Then share what you must with family or guests. The secret to really successful stress busting is to have at least one-third of a gallon left. Leave it in the freezing container and slip it back into the freezer or the freezing compartment of the refrigerator.

Go about your business. Care for your family, friends. Tie up any loose ends of the day that may still be dangling in front of you. Get your bath and go to bed if you are sleepy. The ice cream will hold. Timing has to be right. It'll be fine in the freezer for a week or so. Rest in the knowledge that it's there. Waiting.

What you need at this point is an extremely exhausting day. Real fatigue. The kind you can't shake. The kind that crawls into bed with you at night daring you to close your eyes, reminding you with every breath of all you did not get done during the day, and all that's waiting for you as soon as the sun rises.

NOW! Go find the largest, fluffiest towel you own and go to the freezer. Take out that metal container with your name on it. Remove the top. Wrap the canister in the towel. Retrieve the largest spoon in the kitchen – literally the biggest one you can find that you can slide into the container. Go back to bed. Be sure your pillows are just right. Curl up cross-legged with the frozen treasure cradled in your arms and DIG IN!

You have to trust me here, until you try it for yourself, that is, it is impossible to think about anything else while indulging this elegantly (and secretively). No deadlines. No chores. No relationship issues. Nothing can enter this time if you focus on the phenomenal experience I have prescribed here.

Wiggle every frozen smidgeon all around on your tongue. Taste the chocolate as you have never tasted chocolate. Search for a tiny hunk of banana. Let yourself totally experience the pleasure of every bite. When you are finished, set the towel wrapped container on the floor by the bed. Lie back. Cuddle deep into your pillow and go to sleep with full knowledge that God loves you even more that you have just loved yourself.

Sweet dreams...

Telling It Like It Used To Be – July 2000
I know. Anything could happen. I shouldn't get my hopes up. I should pretend it will be just another day. No big deal.

But I can't. If the Lord's willing and the creek don't rise (and there seems to be little danger of that this summer), I am FINALLY going to hear T. Graham Brown in concert at The Gospel Barn, in LaGrange, Georgia. The Gospel Barn is one of my new favorite places since we moved to the country two years ago.

Guideposts Magazine recently did a cover story on T. Graham, and his wife Sheila, which chronicled his victory over an alcohol problem that dogged his career until five years ago. He gives credit for the victory to God's unconditional love for him, and the love and support of his wife and son.

Brown is a Georgia native and has a sound that is native to nowhere. His music has many times been described as part rhythm & blues, part country, part gospel, and *all* heart. His latest album, "Wine Into Water" features a bit of it all. The title song is about his victory over alcoholism. Brown himself calls the project "the most honest, truest album I've ever done."

I thought I was going to hear the singer perform in Nashville a few years ago. He was slated to offer some late night entertainment at a convention I was attending, but didn't show. They said he was ill.

Now, I'm no concert junkie. Don't really care for crowds at all, in fact. But T. Graham gave a concert in Tallahassee, Florida on Saturday night, February 6, 1988, a concert that I desperately wanted to attend.

I was staying at a hotel a few blocks from Tallahassee Memorial Hospital. As I drove back and forth from the hotel to the hospital, I kept hearing the concert promotions on the radio. My sister and I began to fantasize about escaping from the painful death watch in which we were engulfed to go hear T. Graham sing "Tell It Like It Used To Be."

Of course, we did not leave our father's side. Instead we reminisced about how it "used to be" when we were younger and Daddy was healthy and all was well. In a strange way, T. Graham helped us get through a painful time. And the desire to hear him perform has remained with me.

SO! I have plans once more to hear this gifted performer who spans so many singing styles with such ease.

Now, on another note, I had a call from my sister, Lynda, this morning and we found ourselves in an interesting discussion about how easy it is to misjudge people and how careful we should be about judging folks at all. Then we talked for a minute about how God opens and closes doors. He does that, you know.

And she said to me, "I have a book that I keep readily accessible, near my bed, in fact, because the author has a way of driving home the fact that failure may be God's way of saying you are on the wrong road."

She frequently interviews applicants for jobs with her company. She prides herself on being a good judge of character. Nevertheless, there are those individuals who do not always succeed in her line of work, so they move on. Now, I don't know it for a fact, but I suspect she's wanted to tell more than one individual who has left the company because they found they could not keep up the pace and perform well, "Failure may be God's way of saying 'you're on the wrong road.'"

You might want to chew on that little piece of advice for a while, or share it with someone else who needs to hear it. We are all in this thing called life together, you know. Another's success or failure could very easily be our own.

Some Doors Can't Be Closed – August 2000

We all have doors we want to close, don't we? If we don't slam them immediately, then at some time or another, on down the road, we know we'll eventually close certain doors. Right?

Wrong.

We are what we are. No influence that has touched us ever goes away. From the cradle to the grave we are becoming. We are one with what touches us.

Last week, I ran into a first cousin while I was down in Columbus. Just walked right smack dab into her at Minnie's (about the best eatery in town for down home southern country cooking at lunch time).

I had not seen Theresa for years. That happens when you have as many cousins as I do, and when you let time get away from you.

We reminisced over lunch. I told her about the upcoming T. Graham Brown concert in nearby LaGrange, how I'd wanted to hear him for more than 12 years and how certain I was that I finally was going to be able to close some doors.

She laid down her fork, looked at me, straight into my eyes, and said, "I don't think we ever get to do that."

I could hardly swallow after her comment.

There was a pause in our conversation while the four of us absorbed the weight of her words. We both had a friend with us – friends who were somewhat lost, I suppose, as Theresa and I talked about our past and the pain that never goes away.

One of eight children, she has lost three siblings. She was once in a bad automobile accident in which her sister died, while she lived. Another sister died from cancer. A year later, that sister's son died in an auto accident. And, before all that, a brother had died in an accident. The year her mom died (the same year my dad died) Theresa had decided that God surely would heal Joy (the sister with cancer); so certain she was that He would not take her sister and her mother during the same year.

Wrong.

I feel we can be assured of very little when it comes to knowing what God will and will not do. But that very little makes all the difference.

What is that assurance? I believe we can be certain that God loves us. No matter what. He is not threatened by our anger or intimidated by our questions. He accepts us as we are and loves us unconditionally.

Then it becomes a relationship thing. A matter of coming to the end of ourselves. The end of going it alone, of doing it by ourselves. And a realization that we get back what we put into it.

It's not what, why, when, or even how, that really matters in life. It's who. Who are we sharing it all with? Who do we talk to every day? Who supports us and loves us and is always there for us?

You may think you have no one. You may be able to name a dozen or more folks. But, there again, it's who you are naming that counts.

The most romantic weddings end in divorce more often that we want to admit. Friends move away. Parents pass on. Siblings die. Loved ones can be gone in an instant. There is only one constant. And that is God's unconditional love for us. His desire to walk with us, talk with us, let us lean on Him, let Him care for us.

But it's our choice.

Always, it's our choice. He made us in His image. He understands. He's proud of what we do, and of the wisdom we show when we choose not to do certain things. He doesn't want to take away our right to make choices, or enjoy and experience life in a thousand ways.

Not at all. He just wants to share it with us.

Think about it. Why did, or why would, an omnipotent God need man? Whatever you perceive God to be, if you recognize Him at all, then surely you must recognize Him as the Creator. And if we are created in His image, as I believe we are, then we share with Him a desire for relationships.

Think I'm way off on this one? Maybe. Maybe not. Could it be that God wants our love and companionship just as much as we need His?

I didn't get to close the doors I wanted to close, but I realized something at the T. Graham Brown concert. I realized there's never been a door though which God did not walk with me. And I know now that that's enough.

Setting the Rooster Free – October 2000

I wonder how many confessions I've made in this column over the past 14 years. It's cheap therapy, this space. Today, it's time to come clean again.

It all started when my neighbor, just down the way, who lived in the middle of a pasture, about a quarter of a mile off the road, was preparing to move to Texas. She called me to ask if I knew who might adopt her chickens.

No, not right off the top of my head, I said. Lying. I just needed time to work on Daniel. He's a good sport and the most tolerant husband who ever lived. But the chickens were gonna take some persuasion.

"Honey, you're crazy," he said. "We've had this conversation before. We've had it ever since we bought the property. We've had it enough. I'm not going to have chickens roaming around my yard. There will be chicken _____ everywhere you step. Chickens are nasty and they stink."

It took me a week. I knew I could pull it off. Of course, Guthrie had to give up his dog pen, but we fixed him a nice house under the back porch and he has adapted quite well to his leash. Jack Russells are smart. They know when they've been had. Like husbands.

A week to the day after I had set out to convince Daniel he would love fresh eggs, my neighbor brought over Honey and Beauregard. Honey, named for her color, was beautiful and faithfully delivered the daily egg for months. Beauregard was downright striking. I don't know much about roosters, but his primary color is white with black tail feathers and his head and wings are multicolored. A real beauty.

For months, we all enjoyed Honey and Beauregard. I say "all" – all, that is, except Guthrie. Guthrie was jealous. He ran circles around that 8 X 10 chicken pen, barking and yelping and telling those birds just what he thought of them. Daniel, however, was sold after the first egg – proving once more that I'm always right!

Then a month ago, I went out one morning to feed my pets and found Beauregard pacing up and down. Didn't see Honey at first. When I drew close to the pen and caught sight of what was left of her, I disintegrated. Just a feather covered shell of bones lay there. Of course, feathers were all over the pen, too. Beauregard had lost a few as well. Daniel figures it was probably a mink. We've spotted a couple down by the creek. There was no way a bobcat, raccoon or coyote could have gotten into the pen.

I cried a lot and couldn't eat for two days. Neither could Beauregard. He was quite torn up emotionally. He crowed more often and paced a lot. I watched for a month. During that time, I talked with Daniel repeatedly about giving Beau the run of the place. "He's so lonely now and the pen that once was a love nest has become a prison. He needs to be free."

We discussed our options. We both were concerned about Guthrie's reaction. But we thought the two just might become buddies. So, after much deliberation, we decided to free Beauregard. We are a thousand feet off the road so traffic would not be a problem. And he had stood his ground against whatever critter had devoured Honey. Maybe he was a survivor. We'd see. We agreed last Sunday that I would let Beauregard out on Monday morning when I went out to feed him.

On Monday around 10 a.m., I called Daniel at work. I needed to be assured I could do this thing. Freedom could mean death and I would be a murderer.

Daniel had known I couldn't do it. He had let the bird out at 5:15 that morning before he left for work. "Just go out and see if he's still alive," he said. "And if he isn't, you're not the killer." Like that was going to comfort me. I'd be just as guilty!

Beauregard was alive and strutting like he was king of the hill. Guthrie, on the other hand, was not a happy camper. Five days have passed now and he's adjusting though. Will they ever be buddies? Not hardly, but they are co-existing quite nicely.

I don't know if Beau knows how, in setting him free, Daniel and I made him much more accessible to the prowling varmints of the night. All I know is freedom looks mighty good on that bird. And every time I go out the door, he proudly fluffs up his feathers two or three times in a row and makes this strange, soft, guttural noise that sounds like "thaaaaank youuuu."

And the chicken _____? Well, watch your step if you stop by.

Southern Lady in Black Jeans – December 2000

Just after Thanksgiving, one of the Estes sisters called to invite me to coffee on Saturday, December 9, from 3 to 5 p.m. I mentioned to my would be hostess that I would have company that weekend, but would try to slip out and come to her home for a few minutes.

In the early twentieth century, Gay was a busy cotton production community and home to a prominent cotton merchant, who built a grand two story brick residence which appears to be an absolutely perfect marriage between the Craftsman and Georgian styles. The lovely home is still occupied by his two daughters, Sara and Jane Estes.

My husband had met the two sisters in 1998, just after we moved to this area. They came by our house while they were out campaigning for their niece who was running for public office. I missed them that day, but was welcomed into their home on two occasions earlier this year.

So gracious they are. Well informed. Well educated. Well traveled. And the kicker... they are real southern ladies. A rarity these days.

So, the Saturday came, as did all my company. I'd been cooking for two days previously so I could be free to enjoy the day. I arose quite early and slipped into a favorite pair of black jeans and my best-looking festive red sweatshirt.

It would be a glorious day. I was sure of it. From my early morning time, with just me and my sister, right through our 8 p.m. tram ride through the Fantasy of Lights over at Callaway Gardens. Ah, yes, it would be a great day.

My friend, Betty, arrived around noon. She also had been invited to the afternoon coffee. About 3:30 p.m., she and I slipped out, leaving a house full of guests to fend for themselves. My sister had laid down for a short nap, but my husband assured me he could hold down the fort.

The coffee was unlike any coffee I'd ever experienced in suburbia. I was unprepared for an "event" – perhaps the event of the season. Could be that nothing tops it throughout the year, except maybe the Cotton Pickin' Fair which is held twice a year, in Gay, on the first weekends in May in October.

No cotton bales at the home of the sisters, however, only pressed linen napkins, the finest china, and sparkling silver service amidst a spectacular Christmas theme (that I am told varies every year). There were dozens of women, at least 50 or so at all times, with cars constantly coming and going in the inviting old circular drive.

What a delightful time I had. I met so many ladies. Of course, I can only recall a few names, but it was a beginning. I did talk for a while with one who'd lived in Gay for ten years and another for 14 years. Both acknowledged that they were still "outsiders."

But nobody felt like an outsider on Saturday. Not hardly. Time stood still as the old south arose from the ashes of yesteryear to offer a promise of hope to all who would still be called a southern lady. At least, that's how I felt in my heart.

Of course, no fantasy lasts forever, no matter how long we try to hold it to ourselves. When I returned home, more company had arrived. My sister was graciously attending to all. When I walked through the door her mouth fell open. "Tell me you didn't," she gasped.

"Didn't what?"

"Wear jeans to an afternoon coffee? Tell me you did not!"

"Well, yes, I did."

"I knew I should not have laid down for that nap. I started to say something earlier, ask what you were wearing, drop some hint that perhaps you should change... Did they let you in the door?"

"Well, yes. What's the big deal?"

"What were the other ladies wearing?"

The suede suits and beautiful dresses, diamonds and furs, suddenly flashed far too vividly in my mind's eye! She knew she had me from the look on my face.

"Don't worry. I shouldn't have said anything at all. Most folks know how weird writers can be anyway. Besides, I'm sure your hostesses were "real" ladies."

Did she mean I didn't stand a chance? I didn't dare ask. For a few brief minutes time had stood still, and I had felt like a real southern lady. In my heart, I knew that clothes never did make or break a true southern lady.

In LA, New York or Paris, attire might say all there is to say, but in Gay, Georgia, I was still a lady, even in black jeans.

Building Mansions and Character – March 2001
Who ever would have thought it would turn out to be a Plantation Week? Ah, but it did!

Months earlier, I had accepted an invitation to speak/read at a Literary High Tea slated for Monday, April 22, at the Grand Wisteria Plantation in Greenville, Georgia. Ordinarily, the Grand Wisteria is a romantic Bed and Breakfast with the elegant essence of a bygone era. Soon to open however, is a truly beautiful and intimate special event facility recently constructed behind the main house.

To participate in the High Tea event was enough to make my week really special. The forty ladies in attendance were so very gracious and made me feel like they really enjoyed my work. I just wasn't sure my week could get any better, since such a reception is a really big deal for a writer who stays to herself far too much, according to some who think they know me!

My husband is one of those who thinks he knows me, and he had this idea that I should go to New Orleans with him on the weekend following my lovely experience at the Grand Wisteria. The father of a friend had passed away and the funeral was on Monday. He thought it would be nice for us to drive over together, rest a day, and drive back after the funeral.

Little did I know what lay in store. It was opening weekend of the annual Jazz Festival so a room was hard to come by, though we did find a nice one at the LaFayette Hotel overlooking a beautiful green square just barely off the beaten path. We were within about five miles of the church where the funeral was to be held on Monday morning.

Now, most folks would have no problem passing time in the Big Easy. And I tried to do just that for about three hours on Saturday afternoon after our arrival. Throngs of folks all around us actually looked like they were having fun.

Me? I was wondering if Sybelina or Mablelina (the wild turkeys I feed in my back yard) would make another appearance with their new babies in tow before I returned home. New Orleans was hot. It was crowded. It was loud. What was there to like?

Daniel asked what I'd like to do on Sunday. He knew "resting" in that downtown atmosphere was not going to be an easy accomplishment. I already knew the trees were within driving distance.

The Oak Alley trees, the grandest old live oaks you could ever imagine were calling to me. And so we drove west, out River Road towards all the old sugar plantations. If you don't blink on this drive you will catch a glimpse of some very stately old dwellings, several of which are now Bed and Breakfasts.

You truly must not blink, because the plantation road frontage is very narrow. I am told that the entrances were just that narrow 150 years ago – narrow at the front, deep and wide at the back, to the tune of 1000 to 10,000 acres. The present owners or managers of some of these magnificent southern beauties can trace their roots back to the original owners. Others have changed hands many times with the transfer of ownership being prompted by little more than a bad hand at poker. Can you imagine!?

Most outstanding on my modern day ride along the Mississippi River were the numerous industries. Though sugar cane fields still abound, industry rules! Or maybe it ruled until we reached Oak Alley Plantation.

Nothing could have interfered with the total joy I gained from seeing and touching those gorgeous old oaks. I learned that a settler along around 1700, had built a small house at the site where the present mansion now stands. This settler had the foresight to plant 28 live oak trees in two very well spaced rows. They reached from his house to the Mississippi. It was not until 1839 that

Jacques Telesphore Roman, a wealthy Creole sugar planter, built the present mansion as a summer home for his lovely bride.

Today, Oak Alley is a National Historic Landmark with its antebellum mansion and surrounding 25 acres. Of the original property, 75 acres is now a residential community that surrounds the mansion; 600 acres are leased for sugar cane cultivation, and 450 acres remain virgin woodlands.

Along with experiencing the stately old oaks, I also was privileged to share in the celebration of the life of a stately old man that I'm sorry I never met. As I walked out of St. David's Catholic Church on Monday morning and away from the poignant funeral service of Henry Philip Julien, Sr. I knew that the song "May the Work I've Done Speak For Me" had once more been very appropriately performed.

Some folks build mansions. Others build character. It was clear that Mr. Julien had been a character builder. My trip was complete.

Swamp Gravy – July 2001
"The community that plays together stays together" is a good motto for my home town of Colquitt, Georgia where Swamp Gravy has received international acclaim.

Colquitt is a good town to hail from and I readily claim such roots. I always like to go back. In spite of all the attention the Colquitt/Miller Arts Council has brought down on the little town, I think Colquitt remains relatively unchanged from 30, 40 even 50 years ago.

Just what is Swamp Gravy, and how did the Arts Council put Colquitt on the map in a big way with it? It's Georgia's own Folk Life Play, a continuing storytelling tradition. Though every production is deeply steeped in southern roots, the stories have a universal appeal.

Each spring and fall more than a hundred local and area citizens come together to weave the magic that becomes yet another helping of Swamp Gravy. Hollywood could learn a lesson or two.

Many accomplished southern storytellers refer to their tales as pot likker for the soul. Some of us, blessed to be born and raised in the south, are of the belief that the pot likker is where all the nutrients are after the greens, peas or bean have been consumed. And there's not much that can compare to a good hot piece of corn bread and a cup of pot likker for the belly, or the soul. A southerner also knows that if the pot likker does not fill you up, a few big dollops of gravy on biscuits will do the trick any day.

Thus, the soul gets not only fed, but quite sated, when Swamp Gravy is served at Cotton Hall. That's the renovated cotton warehouse that is now a fully equipped theater. Its state of the art lighting, eye-appealing set design and multi level staging and seating make it a real showcase for the arts. Maybe Broadway could learn a thing or two, as well. From rafters to the floor, the design of the theater makes every seat in Cotton Hall a good one.

Swamp Gravy is professionally written, designed and directed, and a new play is presented every fall. Most of the reserved seats are already sold for this October's production which is performed every weekend in October on Friday, Saturday and Sunday. General admission tickets are available, but I don't think a seat comes with those tickets. Instead, the holder stands quietly among the performers or sits on the edge of the stage. Actually, there are those who boast that the general admission tickets are the very best ones.

The upcoming performance entitled "Swamp Gravy, Love and Marriage" claims to have captured the "heaven and hell" aspect of romance. You would think that's why it's almost sold out, but the truth is you need to buy tickets to Swamp Gravy a year ahead if you want a seat, no matter what the theme.

Why talk about "Swamp Gravy" in this column if it is so hard to get a ticket? Well, like I said, it isn't, if you plan well in advance. But the main reason I am reminded today of the production is I was just down in Colquitt again.

In June, I finally spent a night at Tarrer Inn, something I have wanted to do since I was a little girl. This lovely old hotel sitting on the corner of the town square has always fascinated me. A welcome haven to travelers since 1905, it has never been grander than it is today. Beautifully restored as a labor of love, Tarrer is listed on the National Register of Historic Places and is a winner of the Georgia Trust Award for Historic Preservation. It is owned and operated by the Arts Council. It's worth a trip to Colquitt just to sit on the veranda at Tarrer.

It'll take you back in time and the journey will be grand even if you don't hail from Colquitt. It was the first night my husband and I had ever spent together in the little town. Though we were both born there in the tiny two story brick hospital that has since been torn down, we never met until we were grown.

I'm glad we have similar roots. I'm sure that fact has strengthened our marriage, and with a thirty-third anniversary coming up in mid-August, we are increasingly thankful for everything that has enhanced our relationship. But my Colquitt roots also have given me a firm foundation to stand on as an individual, as well – a truth that was driven home quite poignantly the first time I ever saw Swamp Gravy, and even more so when I spent the night at Tarrer and looked out my second-floor bedroom window towards the cemetery where my grandparents, parents, and so many relatives now rest. I felt safe and slept well.

Fresh Air Bar-B-Que - August 2001

It had been a while since Daniel and I had ridden over, in, and around the Indian Springs and Juliette, Georgia area (home, of course, to the unique southern café made famous in the Fried Green Tomatoes film).

I don't care much for the tomatoes myself – tried them once – that's all it takes for me to know I don't like something edible. People, as in potential friendships, get second, third, sometimes ongoing chances. Not so with food. One knows right off.

Actually it's not fried green tomatoes I don't like. I like them when I fry them, and I love the ones at the Bullock House in Warm Springs (that would be the little town made famous by former President Franklin Roosevelt) where they somehow manage to keep them crispy from frying pan to buffet to plate to mouth (They are awesome! It's quite an accomplishment to keep a fried green tomato crisp for that long!). I just did not like the ones at the Whistle Stop Café on the day I was there. Theirs were limp and greasy, not at all crispy. But, in all honesty, they did taste just like the ones my mama used to fry when I was a child, so that oughta count for something.

While we were in Juliette I did find something I really loved. There's a new candy shop, McCrackin Street Sweets. Pralines, clusters of white and dark chocolate with a great variety of nuts, fudge – all kinds. Oh my!

I shouldn't have gone in there at all, but at least I had the good sense to limit my purchases and share everything equally with Daniel. I have been known to hoard good chocolate, Daniel understands it's real generosity when I opt to share a bite!

By the way, if interested, you can find this candy on the web at www.georgiacandy.com. The fellow who makes the candy has a degree in forestry, mind you, but couldn't make a decent living tending our forests. So he is now an Official Confectioner of the Cherry Blossom Festival and owner of The Popcorn Basket Inc, of which the candy store is a subsidiary. I always find it intriguing to discover how way leads on to way.

We spent the entire afternoon rediscovering the Butts and Monroe County area. Even drove by the old Jarrell Plantation where they charge $5 for a tour. Near the old plantation site is a recently constructed bed and breakfast. Nice.

But guess where we wound up? If you have ever been through Jackson on your way to Macon you probably can guess immediately. Yep, Fresh Air Bar-B-Que. What a treat just to set foot in the place. I exclaimed over the smell immediately when we first walked in and made further comments as Daniel paid for the Barbeque and Brunswick Stew that we planned to take home for supper.

The fellow behind the counter asked me if I'd like to see where the smell was coming from. Sure, I said. He took me over and lifted up this gigantic cover off the smoke pit to reveal at least 15 huge hams. The aroma was awesome as I leaned into for a most unforgettable peek.

Of course, my curiosity is never easily sated, so I had to see where the fire was coming from and how the smoke got to the pit. As I gazed in wonder at the elaborate cooking setup I could see Daniel out of the corner of my eye. I've been bugging him to build us a barbeque pit at home. I knew better, from the expression on his face, than to even ask if he could reproduce a smaller replica of what I was observing.

The old chimney, into which you could easily walk, has been standing on the Fresh Air Bar-B-Que premises since 1929. They are not permitted to use it anymore for their cooking flame so the owners have concocted a smaller fire pit to the right of the fireplace.

This new wood burning area is about three feet high and four feet wide and maybe four to five feet deep. There they keep a constant fire going (what a job!) and the smoke drifts down an eight to ten feet tunnel into the pit where those luscious hams become the barbeque folks that flock there to buy.

It was a really nice excursion. We took home our purchases and made sandwiches, which, along with the stew and potato chips, made a nice Sunday night dinner on our front porch as we watched the sunset. It's not often we have such a relaxing Sunday afternoon.

Usually, we have lots of company on the weekend, which we thoroughly enjoy, so we wouldn't want to make such a Sunday getaway a habit, but every now and then the highway calls, and it's almost always worth answering the call.

Chocolate Sin – September 2001

A friend of mine, who happens to also be on staff at one the newspapers that buys my column, says she always gasps when I announce right off that I am about to do some confessing.

I suspect no formal confessional could ever hold a candle to what this space has been on occasion. I can only hope she's ready for this one. She will recognize right off how it could so easily be she who would have to confess if the same temptation ever came her way.

It's chocolate sin again. But not just any chocolate. Oh, no, not at all. Its Sadie's chocolate – her chocolate pies to be specific.

Sadie is one of Daniel's sisters. She is the sister-in-law that most folks only dream about. She's really pretty amazing in many areas, but when it comes to chocolate pies she is unsurpassed.

For every family occasion she makes two of those pies. There are usually from 20 to 60 folks at a typical family function, depending on the time of the year and the occasion. But she always makes just two pies.

I have been known to cut my sliver prior to eating the main meal. I know what my priorities are. And nobody ever gets two pieces of pie. One, it's so rich you just can't, and two, if you dared try, somebody would swat your hand with a reminder that there has to be enough to go around. Somehow, there always is.

Perhaps I should get on with my story - my confession, that is.

Last weekend we had the whole clan at our place. There were 34 people. I made brownies and oatmeal/chocolate chip/walnut combo cookies, both of which I thought would be fun-eating and easy-snitching throughout the day. Sadie made and brought a banana pudding and her two chocolate pies.

I'm not sure just how it happened. But somehow, there was a whole pie left. Unsliced. Untouched. A whole pie!

I suppose Sadie must have picked up on the distress I thought I was hiding at the thought of that pie leaving my house and going back home with her.

Miraculously and compassionately, she offered. "MJ, why don't you just slide this pie out of my serving dish and keep it. I need to take the dish with me, but I don't really want to take that pie back home"

I'm no fool. I didn't even pretend to politely protest. I quickly and ever so quietly took that pie plate and did exactly as she suggested. Then I slipped it into the refrigerator. I prayed nobody had witnessed my subtle action.

The next day, everybody was finally gone. The house was quiet. Daniel was out. The pie was calling my name.

With tremendous respect, I retrieved it from its refrigerated place of hiding. I sat it on the counter and debated. Would I? Could I? What would happened if I...? No, I absolutely could not eat the whole thing. Well, actually I probably could, but I just couldn't – certainly not all at one sitting or even in one day. So I devised a plan.

I cut the pie into eight equal pieces. Every day for the rest of the week (it was the "week" following Labor Day weekend and it started on Tuesday) I would have a sliver for breakfast and another sliver for lunch.

I followed my plan. I have no regrets. No guilt. No remorse. Really no need for confession now that I think about it. Perhaps I'm just gloating.

At one point there was a twinge of something that remotely resembled guilt. Maybe it was when I remembered that though the pie was well hidden, the scales were still in plain view.

Then I remembered a physician I interviewed one time. I had asked her about her own lifestyle and specifically, I had asked what her children ate for breakfast. "Usually cake," she had said.

She saw the expression on my face. "Well, cake is healthier than a lot of the cereals out there."

I can only imagine how her kids would appreciate Sadie's homemade (crust and all) chocolate pie!

Gene and Jimmy – February 2002
Several years ago, I wrote a column about my Aunt Maybelle Giles – in which I said nobody can hold a candle to the likes of her.

That was before I spent the day with her sons, Gene and Jimmy, on a quail hunt, or shoot, or never-to-be-forgotten excursion of sorts. In other words, I made a memory!

Gene and Jimmy are 64 and 61 respectively, going on 19 and 16, respectively, and eternally. They are extremely good-looking.

And I suppose, to date, that was the one thing that I consistently thought of when the two came to mind.

I readily concede now that my shallow thoughts did not begin to do justice to these two rambunctious offspring of the south.

I must spare you many details of my day with the two, as this paper could never print some of the stories I heard. Daniel had hunted with them the day before I joined them and he assures me they all cleaned up their act for me! In all honesty, I wish I had been a fly on the wall the day before.

And what a wall it was! The day started out in a 75 foot "shed" as they call it. A roaring fire in an old potbellied stove greeted me. I sat before it on what appeared to be some kind of plow or disc – what do I know? – that had been converted into a bar stool of sorts. Red-neck wind chimes tinkled off to my left.

Thank heaven there were no horses or mules. The thought of riding in a buggy behind them all day held no appeal to me. I'm a four-wheeling woman through and through and was very appreciative of the jeep that would pull our wagon that day. Jimmy built the wagon. As a young cousin, SEVERAL years younger, I always thought he could do anything. Now I know he can.

We pulled ourselves away from the warm wood heater for the guys (that would be Gene, Jimmy and Jimmy Moree, their buddy) to give me a tour of the flight house. Picture a more sophisticated, better looking and tad more intelligent threesome, as in Curly, Larry and Mo... and you can begin to imagine how my day unfolded.

That flight house was the more than 100 foot long pen where the birds are raised. To be invited into it was an honor. Some degree of reverence is what I found myself feeling as I observed the threesome at work. The boys (forget age here!), tenderly shooed or herded or maneuvered the birds toward the light.

That would be the light in the tunnel that led to the room where they were held until Moree went in there to shoo them into the chutes through which they walked to the cages in which they were loaded for the ride to the fields.

If you are an animal rights activist, don't even think about going there with me. Like Daniel said, "At least, they were about to give them a flying chance."

And that they did! I didn't shoot. Didn't even carry a gun. I rode in the jeep with Gene all day. He's the doc, as in M.D. He's had a number of celebrities down for hunts in conjunction with Quail Unlimited activities and they always want to know what he does. He prefers not to say.

As I listened to him talk, it appeared that country music stars are among his favorite past guests. I wondered how Daniel and I were measuring up.

Gene likes to play the guitar and sing, too. He used to perform live at some kind of Saturday night shindig in Panama City, when he owned a condo down there.

I want to try to describe for you the moment by moment action of the day, but I can't. I don't know how. The threesome kept teasing Daniel and insisted that if he would put his shotgun in his right hand he might could impress them a bit. But my leftie did me proud.

I think what most fascinated me was watching the dogs perform. Observing their different personalities. Feeling their excitement. You can do that, you know, really feel what they feel if you let yourself. I could.

I let myself feel everything, to the fullest. It was the fourteenth anniversary of my dad's death. At last, I was making a memory that could compete positively with that February day in 1988.

Gene had been my dad's doctor. He had done all he could before he had sent him back to the Tallahassee heart specialists. I have cried on February 7, every year since my Daddy died. I didn't cry this year. Some hearts can't be healed. Some can.

Soup and Lacy Corn Bread – February 2002

I am considering changing my ways. Just "considering" at this point, just thinking about it. I'm no where near ready to make a decision. So let's talk about the way I do it and perhaps that will help me to decide if I will seek to know more or better cookery organization.

First off, there are no menus. Not since my first year of marriage when I didn't know how to cook beans. Beans or anything else for that matter, except biscuits. I learned biscuits in fourth grade 4-H and make an awesome biscuit to this day, with lots of variations from my basic non-existent recipe. Yep, it's a memory thing and I never measure.

So how do I cook? With no menus? The same way I write or draw or decorate. I use whatever is on hand. "Whatever is on hand" usually means whatever was on special the last few times I was at the grocery. You guessed it, I will not pay prime price for anything.

So, it's close to meal time and I go to the pantry, freezer or refrigerator about thirty minutes to an hour before time to eat, shuffle this or that around, and come out with whatever strikes my fancy. In doing so, I came up with an awesome potato soup just a few weeks ago.

I had some cubed ham in the freezer, left over from baking a smoked ham a couple of weeks back. There were potatoes in the pantry begging to be cooked. There were several cans of cream of mushroom soup on the shelf.

Onions were in the bottom drawer of the refrigerator. I pulled out a few baby carrots to chop, and a stalk of celery as well. That's when I saw the sour cream. I decided it would become the "secret" ingredient for my potato soup. I threw everything together as it felt right, no measuring, and let it all simmer for an about 45 minutes.

Then I fried the lacy corn bread, another one of my specialties. It took years to get the hang of it, but now I can hang my lace out with the best of them.

That brings me back once more, to all those folks who have real systems. Their own systems may serve them just fine, but I have a system of sorts, too. Organization is not at the center of it, but some darn good vittles find their way out of whatever it is that does center me, so I don't think I will do any major changing anytime soon.

Maybe at another time, on another day, I will reconsider. For now, I feel creative and I hear my kitchen calling. And by the way, I probably have not thrown out more than five specially created concoctions from nothing (nothing meaning throwing things together without a plan) in all my years of cooking.
In fact, as the years go by I am learning to like me and all my ways more and more. And my lacy cornbread? I like it so much I'm willing to share.

Lacy Cornbread Recipe:
Stir water and self-rising cornmeal mix together. For years I used White Lily, but last year I discovered Three Rivers, which is awesome! Don't ask, I already told you I don't measure. Just get a two cup measuring cup if that comforts you and pour maybe three-fourths of a cup of cornmeal mix in it. Now add water very slowly, at a trickle, directly from the faucet. Stir as you add the water. You are going for something close to the consistency of tomato juice.

Heat a large black iron skillet. Nothing else will do. Pour in Canola oil to cover the pan, just to lightly cover it (a few tablespoons). If you tilt the pan, the oil should gently slide to the side. The trick is to have just enough oil in the pan that the cornbread will sizzle (like making pancakes) when you pour in a miserly dollop that spreads out no smaller in circumference than a coffee cup top and no bigger than a saucer.

Brown it on one side on medium high heat, then flip and brown the other side. You will master the art the day that the outer edges want to fall off if you are not very careful as you turn the bread and the inner center is not at all mushy anymore.

You can fry three to four pieces at the time and you must add a tad more oil between each frying. Don't let the little crispies stay in the pan between fryings or they will burn and smoke up the house. Once you get the hang of it, you will never look for the cracker box again when having soup. Or peas. Or beans. Or turnips.

Plus, if you are lucky, you will begin to appreciate the secrets of those of us who grew up on cornbread and whatever vegetables we "put up" for the year. Making do with the grocery store specials and whatever I still put up from the garden each year, is just downright fun, so I say, why spoil a perfectly good system?

My Mama's Family – April 2002

"Would you like anything from the buffet while I'm up?"

"Yes, I'd like a piece of that chocolate cake."

"There's only one slice left."

"I'll take it," Betty said.

Gasps went up around the room.

"I know! Mama always told me not to take the last piece of anything, but along about the time I turned 50, I started taking the last piece of anything I wanted."

Laughter rang out in the extended dining area. Most folks in that never to be forgotten setting identified. I, who have been eating dessert FIRST for years, saw much wisdom in the revelation that had been laid out before us.

I suspect there are, in all families, never to be forgotten moments packed with extraordinary tidbits of wisdom, joy, peace and comfort. Moments we hold to our breast, deep in the corners of our hearts, for times when we no longer are surrounded by those we love and those who love us.

I am most blessed. No one who has come before me, or who will follow after me, can ever know more joy than I have known in more ways than I can count. It is awkward to make that claim, knowing how much pain and suffering there is in the world. It is my claim, however, and I make it reverently.

You see, I come from a really big family and family is where it's at! There is no end to what "it" can teach you. The varieties of ways in which "it" can sustain you, restore you, fortify you, and empower you also are endless.

It is said that we all may be subject to fifteen minutes of fame sooner or later. I don't know about that, but if I ever did make any claim to fame I would want that claim to somehow revolve around my having been born in Miller County, specifically Colquitt, Georgia.

That's real important because if you are from Miller County, you can always go home again. And going home again should not be taken lightly.

It is not to be confused with knowing where you've come from. That's important, too. It helps you to get where you are going. But to actually be able to go home again is a rare and precious thing.

I went home to Colquitt yet again this past weekend to celebrate Aunt Benonia's passing. My family does not just bury folks. A funeral is really only incidental to the way we celebrate the exit our loved ones make from the bodies they live in while on earth, although the funerals are indeed something to talk about!

Yes, Aunt Benonia is the one I wrote about a year or so ago. She's the one who – due to a long, long illness – had experienced more "dyings" than any other family member amongst my clan.

It was on April 17 that she finally left this earth. Well.... actually, she may not have left until after the service. She wanted real bad to hang around for it, and if there was any way possible, I'm sure she did. What's more, I'm sure she enjoyed it! I know I did. Don't think I've ever enjoyed anybody's dying celebration quite so much.

There are the throngs of friends and relatives that come and go. There's an endless supply of food and drink brought in by friends and neighbors. The children quickly and easily figure out how to entertain themselves.

Hugs, laughter, tears abound. Memories rule. They carry you. They sustain you. They become you. Thus the never-ending cycle of life goes on. And in that weak moment when the memories are blurred and you can't quite feel that hug you need so much, then it's okay if you want to go for the last piece of chocolate cake. Ain't no mama, dead or alive, gonna slap your hand 'cause they've been there, too.

The Underwear – April 2003

It all started with the early morning news of the death of yet another Marine and still more civilian casualties in Iraq. My heart seems to break often. I pray for the safety of our troops. I pray for guidance for our president and other leaders. I pray that the people of Iraq soon will come to know well freedom and wisely accept the responsibilities that come with it. And I cry sometimes, as I go through my routines of daily living.

After my first dose of morning news I usually flip the TV to a music channel. On this particular morning, I choose Classic Country which sometimes relaxes me and where I feel I will be safe from The Dixie Chicks and other equally insensitive music celebrities. As I seek a brief escape from war and its cruel realities, I suddenly hear the voice of Mo Bandy coming over the airwaves: "Let me watch my children play, and see what they become, Lord don't let that cold wind blow, 'til I'm too old to die young." Truly there is no escape from the reality of the ultimate sacrifice that our soldiers may be called on to pay.

...Suddenly I gasped! "Oh, Lord, what did I do this time?!" I gasped. I looked around the bathroom. Status quo. I checked his bedside table. His ID badge and wallet were gone. As they should be. His belt was missing from the chair where it hangs. That's good. I went to the coffeepot. And there sat the problem.

A can of soup was too much for him! What was I to do?

I called his office. Thankfully, no voice mail during this time of crisis. When he answered, I asked how he was doing. He said fine. I asked about the soup.

Well, I don't have a can opener out here, so I didn't bring it.

What had led to this moment was the healthy diet I had put him on about four weeks ago. I had been making salads the night before and leaving them in the fridge for him to grab as he goes out the door shortly after 4 a.m.

We all know that 4 a.m. can be a strain for anyone, even a morning person, which he is. So he relies heavily on routine. And that routine must not be messed with. If it is, in any way, and I will spare you past details, then he almost always forgets something. Like his wallet, or his ID badge, or his portfolio.

But never his underwear.

So as he explains why he did not take the soup, I listen carefully. I say I will buy him a can opener to keep at work. I explain that the soup was full of nutrients, different from what he'd been getting in the salads, and besides I was out of lettuce.

Then I asked if he was comfortable.

Well, yes.

I mean, are you doing okay? I can drive into Atlanta if you need me to bring anything to you.

What are you getting at?

The underwear, I whisper.

He roars with laughter. After which, he assures me he is wearing underwear. But he knows immediately why I'm worried. Says he remembers crawling out of bed, stripping off his underwear, tossing them in the hamper, opening the drawer and getting new underwear, placing them on the bathroom counter by his sink, taking a shower, and then he cannot explain why he went back to the chest and pulled out a second pair of briefs.

He is absolutely positive however, as he sits at his desk sixty miles away, that he is wearing underwear and it's clean!

Comforted, I return to my own work. I'm still laughing. I feel that it's okay to laugh. Maybe that's why today's troops and thousands upon thousands before them, have laid their lives on the line: for us, for you and me to be free to laugh, to be real, to just freely be.

It could be that I'm taking my freedom a bit far in assuming it's okay to tell you about Daniel's underwear. I recall how my older son once told me he "figured it would be easier to get forgiveness than permission." Hope that line works for me.

The underwear incident was four days ago. I'm still crying and laughing. And I'm praying. I realize that God hears me though the laughter and the tears. I whisper yet another thank you to Him for our troops and pray fervently that those they seek to liberate will soon be free to celebrate the everyday moments of their lives with the same lighthearted laughter I am blessed to know.

The 2003 Class Reunion – October 2003

The MCHS Class of 1966 came together this past weekend in Warm Springs for the reunion of a lifetime. We normally get together every five years and it's always fun, but something was different this time, and I suspect that the happy, unique success of our weekend had little, if anything, to do with human efforts.

The White House Inn was the setting. Mac's Barbecue and Steak House did the catering. Rene Hawkin of Columbus, provided the music on Saturday night. And one of our own, Bill Lawrence, came out of his shell on Friday night and wowed us with guitar and song! As perfect as was the part played by all I mention here, the real secret to the success of the weekend clearly was God's grace.

Early in the six month planning period, I had sent out a 40 part questionnaire. Many courageous souls attempted to answer it. A couple of folks actually answered EVERY question. I was not that brave.

Then I took all the returned answers and spent several weeks composing a memory book to beat all memory books. The effort has blessed my life immeasurably, and I'm getting the impression that it has positively impacted other lives as well.

Now, I can't tell you in this column what's in the book. I can, however, briefly tell you a story.

By the time my family moved to Mitchell County and I started attending classes with students destined to be the Class of 1966, we had lived in 18 homes. Most folks would probably say houses, but my family had a way of making each dwelling a home.

In Mitchell County, in the Lester Community, we lived for one year in a six room home (with a bath) which I loved. Then we moved again and lived for two and a half years in a four room house. All nine of us. With no bathroom. I was ashamed.

I missed out on a lot in high school because I never let myself get close to the kids who I thought "had it all." The nice houses.

The family farms. The good looking clothes. Roots. Stability. Everything I thought I did not have. Ah, the blind, self-centered foolishness of youth... How do we survive it?

Actually, my introduction to Camilla, Georgia came before we moved there. My dad worked full time at Turner Air Force Base, in Albany. In the afternoons, after "work", he did past due debt collections for a local Collection Agency. Then on Friday nights, and all day Saturday, he would cut meat in a grocery market that eventually closed down.

He heard that a butcher was needed at a little corner grocery just off the square in Camilla, so he began to drive down there from Albany to work on the weekends. I went with him and sold chocolate covered peanuts from behind the candy counter at the dime store when I was 13. That was where I first began to meet the kids who were to be part of the Class of 66 – kids whose influence would touch my life, and indirectly, yours, perhaps, for all eternity.

During our three day reunion, late Saturday night, well past midnight, Vicki put on a CD of her daughter's music for us to hear. We are all proud mamas and daddies these days! From that Cassie Clements CD rang out "Daddy's Hands."

As I quickly eased myself away from the crowd, Sherry joined me, and held me. Tears flowed. For the first time, I told a classmate about my daddy's hardworking hands. After I, the oldest of the seven children, left home, Daddy went to Seminary and became an ordained minister. He still worked at the base (civil service), but preached on Wednesday nights, Sundays, and at any revival service where folks would listen. The hands that had cut the meat which fed our bodies eventually held a Bible from which he fed souls.

When daddy died, all his earthly belongings, except his clothes, were left in a desk in the little study of the parsonage that was furnished by the church he pastored at the time. Yet, on the best day ever, the greatest minds at the New York Stock Exchange could never put a value on all that I have inherited from my daddy.

One classmate asked "why here?" in reference to the location that had been chosen for the reunion. I did not really know the answer until now. But as all the emotional dust settles, I'm realizing that back home the little circles we all so foolishly drew around ourselves, such a long time ago, may have still wielded some influence, even today. So I figure God drew a bigger circle and took us all in as we came together atop a beautiful mountain in Warm Springs, Georgia.

The Vicks – December 2003

They say confession is good for the soul. Normally, I don't put much store in what "they say." But, every now and then, they hit on the truth about a thing or two.

The Bible tells us that pride goes before destruction. Now I have no desire to self destruct. So I try to watch out for that bad kind of pride. Well, for six weeks now, if the truth be told, I've been wallowing in that bad kind of pride. And it's time to 'fess up.

There are girls who emulate their moms from the get-go. Daughters who are so pleased to look like, sound like, and act like their moms. Since I'm not reclining on a high dollar shrink's black couch, I won't go into all the details about how and why I'm not one of those daughters. Suffice it to say, I do not choose deliberately to look like, sound like, or act like my Mama.

Now, I'm not saying she is not worthy of such. But I have chosen all my life not to act like her. I mean, right down to the point of rebellion, I will not be like my mama! That, however, is not my confession of the day. That's just the truth.

So what is it that I have to say? And why is it so hard for me?

Well, not only am I about to admit my mama was right about something, I'm about to tell you my that baby sister is, too. This hurts. So, let me just spit it out: Vick's VapoRub works!

I am prone to laryngitis and bronchitis (yes, like my mom) and she kept me bathed in the stuff while I was growing up. If I sneezed, the "Vicks Salve" was brought out. Not that it was ever put up. Mama kept it at the ready for whatever ailed anybody.

Sneezes, coughs, congestion, sore aching muscles – absolutely, they all got treated with Vick's! I swore, if I ever lived to get out of that house, I would never own a jar of the stinking stuff.

Then, about a year ago, my baby sister was staying with me for a few days and she asked where I kept the "Vick's Salve." I proudly informed her that the only jar of that mess that had ever been in my house was that which Mama had brought with her on visits over the years. That's what I told Baby Sis. Yes, proudly.

She said I was crazy. That she could not live without her Vick's. That Mama would roll over in her grave if she knew I was talking like that.

Okay... so, for six months last year I had laryngitis. From mid December of 2002 to mid year, 2003. My doctors and I tried everything before it finally began to let up. Then, on the second Monday of October, it hit again. My voice faded. Congestion set in. I don't know what possessed me, but I went out and bought a jar. Yes, a jar of Vicks VapoRub. It worked. My voice was back within a week.

Then I tried it on Daniel's aching shoulder. The one he aggravates when he shoots his bow or sits at a computer for an hour. It worked.

Then the ultimate test. Now, I don't recall Mama ever using her Vicks for a cold sore (fever blister), but I've been prone to cold sores since childhood. My cold sores are ten dayers. Occasionally, one will run its course within seven days, but usually they are with me a full ten days. Until... Oh, this is so hard to admit! Until I tried my Vicks. On November 25, 2003, when I first felt the cold sore coming on, I started applying my Vicks. Five days later it was gone. Gone!

Vick's VapoRub works! I intend to never be without it again. I'm thinking about having an upstairs jar and a downstairs jar. Maybe even a jar for the truck and jar for the car.

I'm sure Mama is rejoicing on the other side of Glory that I have finally seen the light. I can only imagine how my Baby Sister will gloat. I reckon I will just be ready to remind her that gloating is a first cousin to that pride thing.

The Servant – February 2004

I don't think I ever really grasped the meaning and gravity of the word "paradigm" until I read "The Servant" by James C. Hunter. I now understand that "paradigms are simply psychological patterns, models, or maps we use to navigate our way through life. Our paradigms can be helpful and even life saving when used appropriately. They can, however, become dangerous if we assume our paradigms are never-changing and all-encompassing truths and allow them to filter out the new information and the changing times that are coming at us throughout life. Clinging to outdated paradigms can cause us to become stuck while the world passes us by." (from the book)

I'm not averse to change. If you know me, and you probably do by now, you know I'm not opposed to switching gears, jumping ship, rewriting books... I really am very open to a better way/s. In fact, sometimes I ride the wings of change in absolute glee. BUT, I have my moments when I will sit like a dinosaur on top of the biggest rock around and dare anyone to try to move me.

Like all aspects of our personalities, that can be a good thing and a bad thing. Sometimes my dinosaur on top of the rock activity might be called brave and courageous, even insightful, I suppose. At other times, such behavior is indicative of nothing but old-fashioned stubbornness.

Dear readers, let me assure you, there is a tremendous difference between being boldly courageous and being downright stubborn. I imagine you already know that because the difference is usually blatantly clear. In fact, some of you may be wondering why I would even relate the two adjectives, much less tie them almost synonymously together.

Actually, I never would have done that until I read "The Servant." It's a simple book. An easy read. One I did not want to put down once I started it.

My guess is that this book would never have been published if author James C. Hunter, a labor relations training consultant, was not a popular public speaker and trainer. You can check him out at www.jameshunter.com.

I don't know him. Have never met him. Haven't even spoken to him by phone. Didn't need to before I wrote this column. In this case, the book stands on its own. But I know enough about the publishing industry to know that this book is like hundreds of other good books whose authors are not "out there" so publishers seldom take their manuscripts seriously. I'm glad Hunter is actively in the public eye so that Prima Publishing (a division of Random House) did take him seriously and did recognize his work for the highly marketable product it was/is.

If you should decide to read "The Servant," be prepared for just a wee bit of discomfort. Chances are you will see yourself in all its characters. I did.

A friend recently recommended "The Servant" to me. A friend who never fails to get it right. I hope you have a friend like that. One who listens well. One who hears what you say and what you do not say. A friend who is linked up with God so that God can whisper in his or her ear and fill in the blanks when you don't have the courage or time to share all the truth that needs sharing.

It's kind of like having a three way conference call when you talk to a friend who knows God. Then later, when it's just you and God, or her or him and God, then the conversation continues, and truth…well, truth, and all its many layers, just keeps on rising to life's assorted surfaces.

I understand that Hunter has a new book coming out in June, 2004 entitled "The World's Most Powerful Leadership Principle: How to Become a Servant Leader."

I can't wait to read it and consider more of his insights. Hunter's exploration, to date, of the principles of management and leadership is quite timely for today's world. Truly this author has shaken the foundation of some of my old, tried and true (?), paradigms.

All Things Jesus – February 2004

One thing about it, Mel Gibson's movie, The Passion, sure has revived an interest in all things Jesus. And when you are looking at all things Jesus, division is a word that immediately comes to mind. But Jesus Christ did not teach an exclusionary or divisive message.

Jesus is reported to have summed up His ultimate message like this: "The first commandment requires that you shall love the Lord your God with all your heart, all your soul and all your mind. And the second commandment clearly requires that you love your neighbor as yourself."

That's it. That's what it appears Jesus was, and is, all about.

No more. No less. In fact, He Himself said you could hang all the law and all the prophets on those two commandments. No pomp, circumstance and fluff. Nothing to set apart his followers except love, the active "do unto others as you would have them do unto you" kind of results oriented love.

I have learned much about Jesus from church attendance over the years. But, if the truth be told, I have learned much that I have chosen to unlearn. I have come to realize that the Jesus story is so much simpler than many folks, especially those caught up in organized religion, make it out to be.

I see it like this: There was a Creator God, or Eternally Existent Being ("I AM"). He made man. He made rules. He loved His creation. The creation broke the rules. The penalty was death. Jesus, who was with God at Creation said, "Don't kill them. I know you love them. Let me go down and die for them. Let me take their punishment. Let me redeem them." And when the timing was right that is exactly what he did.

Think about it like this. A nine year kid labors for weeks building a little boat. He takes it to a stream to play and the boat, which is so eager to find out how it can perform in the setting for which it was created, quickly gets caught up in the water currents and very independently floats away from its creator.

Many weeks later, the little kid is playing at a friend's house and he sees the boat amongst a pile of toys and clutter in the friend's room. It's all scratched up, broken in a couple of places, but recognizable. He wants his boat back. The friend says "no, it's mine, I found it."

The creator of the boat goes home and retrieves all his money from his piggy bank, goes back to the friend's house and buys back his boat. He repairs all the broken places and makes it like new again, then sets it free once more in the streams of life to be all the little boat is was created to be. Created, redeemed, repaired and stronger than ever, this time the little boat which has come to appreciate and love its maker, waits for that maker to offer guidance or lovingly lead.

So, maybe the created ones (you and me) were too eager to try our wings to take time to even acknowledge our Maker in the beginning. Maybe we were too big for our britches as elders of yesteryear might have said. Then again, maybe the Creator decided all those rules were just too complex for some of us, and that's why Jesus said we don't have to go there. He really simplified the whole picture with those instructions to just love God with all our being and love our neighbor the same way we love ourselves.

So, how does one become a Christian? Believe the Jesus story. Admit there were rules and we broke them. Ask God to forgive us for breaking the rules. Ask for the Holy Spirit (God and Jesus combined) to come into our heart and life and guide us and keep us. It's really a no-brainer, folks. It's just a matter of connecting with the One who wrote the Manual, and letting His spirit guide us in our thought and action. For Christians, the man Jesus – His life, His death, His Spirit – is the bridge to such a connection.

I suppose I am thankful for The Passion and anything that stirs us to think and talk about all things Jesus. But just thinking and talking is not enough. Jesus is about being out in the midst of life and actively loving God, loving and respecting ourselves as His creation, and loving others as we love ourselves.

IN CLOSING

As I apply the last bit of editing to this collection of columns pulled from among nearly a thousand that I have written since 1986, I do so with mixed feelings. When I changed careers in 1986, and left my job as a nurse to try my hand as a writer/publisher, little did I know all the ways I would be permitted to continue to take the pulse of the people. It has been my privilege to not only take the pulse, but to almost touch the beating hearts of so many people with whom I have interacted over the years. To pick one person, or even make a short list of persons, who have most influenced me with the rhythms of their lives would be impossible. I can say but one thing with absolute certainty to all whose paths have crossed mine:

You and yours have touched the lives of me and mine
and we are changed forever.

Thus it is in life. We touch one another daily, hourly, moment by moment. I suspect when it comes right down to it, life may actually be measured in seconds: the seconds that it take to smile, wink, laugh, give a hug, whisper a prayer, offer encouragement. Nothing is ever as complicated as we try to make it. It is enough that we live and love well. And what would be the secret to accomplishing that? Ah, to live well, that's easy – all we have to do is do what only we can do and do it with all our might.

Did you know that the "do unto others as you would have them do unto you" theme of the Christian faith manifests itself in every major religion? It may be worded differently, like "what you send out into the lives of others comes back into your own," but it's there. To some extent, every faith teaches us to treat others the way we want to be treated. When we seek to love others the way we love ourselves, then you and yours, me and mine... we start to become one. The world will be a better place when we resolve to base our actions on that one common principle. To recognize the theme is a beginning. With such recognition must come a willingness to act. With you and yours, and me and mine, working together, there will be no limit to what we can accomplish. Ah, what a glorious adventure it is that awaits those willing to work together to do what only we can do.

Until later,
Mary Jane Holt
March 15, 2004

What Only You Can Do

"and leave undone forever
what only you can do"

words which haunt me ever
as daily I am pulled
tossed to and fro
always on the go
demands here ... expectations there
so I stand still...
though I want to move to somewhere
but where is somewhere?
and why must I go there?
there is so much I want to do, to say
someday
but when is someday?
and will I know it when it comes?
direction is unclear
a low and winding road beckons
a lovely valley lies below
the ocean calls, the mountains, too
and oh! how I want to go!
but yon path looks smooth and straight...
so, I linger here to await
a word from You
to join the crowd seems right
when "they say" we can win
if I join the fight
and perhaps we could win
a battle, maybe two
but war will wage on
and what will it all matter
when I face You
if I have left undone forever
what only I could do?